Suffering and the Love of God

The Book of Job

Roger Forster

Dedication

I dedicate this book to my near life-long friends Barbara and Colin Lloyd. They have known me virtually all my ministry days of serving Christ full time in his gospel. Their hospitality, friendship and love have been overwhelming and Christ-filled through my varying phases of service. Not least have I appreciated them, and thanked God for them, when I have walked through those areas of life for which Job is well known, areas of pain which we all encounter in our earthly existence.

Barbara is now with Christ, and Colin who walked with her through her last illness is alone, and has experienced his own 'Job' time; but he shares Job's hope of blessing for eternity. Both were, and I believe still are, concerned that some of my understanding of God's truth and ways are preserved for others in the future. Barbara was trained in theology, and her teaching produced some highly successful students by whom she was invariably loved. She loved the truth of God's word, and together with Colin and their family has sacrificed to help this and others of my books to be written and published. My wife Faith and I continue to appreciate and be inspired by Colin and Barbara's love, sacrifice, and the many lovely memories shared – some Job-like, but many more very happy, and all in Christ Jesus.

Since writing the above, a long time friend and erstwhile colleague when he worked in London, Rob Lacey, has also passed into the presence of the Lord. He gave me permission to use his parable on Job in the appendix of this book. I also wish to pay tribute to this well loved creative artist whose work was able to communicate effectively to our contemporary culture, not least through his much acclaimed *Street Bible*. His courage and persistent faith during a prolonged battle with cancer also reflected Job and the message of his book. Sandra his wife who fought with him remains in our hearts and prayers.

I would also like to acknowledge three books which have particularly enriched my meditation on Job as I wrote my own; *The Answer of Jesus to Job* by Campbell Morgan, *Job* by H. L. Ellison and *Job* by J. E. Hartley.

Contents

Foreword

A new book by Roger Forster is always to be welcomed. His previous publications lead us to expect that this volume will be stimulating, biblically based, provocative and probably controversial. And this treatment of the book of Job does not disappoint! It sets out to tackle a problem that all thinking men and women, and Christians in particular, wrestle with – why bad things happen to good people. For the atheist and the unbeliever, this is not a problem. There is no God and we all suffer in the world we have made and that's the end of it. But the Christian believes in the Creator God who made the worlds and sent His Son Jesus Christ to be the saviour of mankind. Since the Bible tells us that God is loving, omnipotent and omniscient, then we do have questions and those questions are what theologians label theodicy – how do we reconcile a loving God with all the pain and disasters and tragedies that are in the world? John Milton, in Paradise Lost, set about to answer this question and described it as justifying the ways of God to man.

Roger Forster believes that a study of the book of Job will help us with this great challenge to faith. Job had God's testimonial that he was a holy and righteous man, yet the most fearful tragedies struck him. All his children were killed, his possessions were lost and he was struck down with a loathsome disease. Job cried out to God but could find no answers to his prayers. While the reader of the book knows what is going on, Job didn't know. He wrestled with God in the depths of despair and longed for death to escape his mental torment and bodily pain. Then his three 'friends' arrived and in three cycles of argument blamed Job for being so blind and stubborn. Could he not see the obvious answer? He was suffering because he had sinned and that is all there was to say.

This book takes on the arguments of Job's 'comforters' and exposes them. It is not so much that they are wrong; rather their well-rehearsed arguments simply don't apply in Job's situation. Job is a righteous man and his suffering is not because of his sin. In a very compelling and fascinating way, Mr Forster characterises the theologies of Job's friends as experiential (Eliphaz), traditional (Bildad) and rational (Zophar). But none of these theologies help Job because they represent what might be described as 'closed systems'. All of them have truth in them but none of them has the whole truth. None of these approaches have answers to Job's questions. The author writes from a theological position closest to that described these days as 'open theism', albeit qualified in his case. Above, beyond and in the universe is a God of love. His great loving purposes for all His creation are not threatened by hidden agendas or absolute and rigid secret decrees. Just as at the end of the book God did not answer all the questions Job asked, so it is with us. God comes to us, as to Job, with lavish grace and the revelation of that almighty love is the guarantee that we are not at the mercy of fate, or chance, or whim, or blind, rigid justice.

I warmly recommend this fine exposition of the book of Job and its very practical and down-to-earth day-to-day application. Roger Forster writes with conviction, with clarity, with passion and always with relevance. Theologically sound, exegetically enlightening and well illustrated from Scripture, this book will prove to be particularly helpful in the ministry of pastoral counselling.

Revd Dr Herbert B McGonigle

Senior Lecturer in Historical Theology, Church History & Wesley Studies, Nazarene Theological College Manchester

For there is hope for a tree,
When it is cut down, that it will sprout again,
And its shoots will not fail.
Though its roots grow old in the ground.

Job 14:7

1

The Problem of Suffering

Job's Innocence

> *There was a man in the land of Uz, whose name was Job,*
> *and that man was blameless, upright, fearing God, and*
> *turning away from evil. (Job 1:1)*

Job was the best man of his time; he did not need humbling in
God's judgment—God thought the world of him. Just in case we
missed it the first time around, God reaffirms it himself in verse 8:

> *And the Lord said to Satan, 'Have you considered My*
> *servant Job? For there is no one like him on the earth,*
> *a blameless and upright man, fearing God and turning*
> *away from evil.'*

From God's point of view, therefore, he did not set about Job with punishment, chastisement and pain in order to bring Job to a place where he would be humbled. That view of the story is fallacious. This saga concerning Job and his suffering is one that is far, far deeper than that less than profound view, even though it is a popular one.

If you or I sin a lot, we should not be surprised if we hurt ourselves a lot. If I walk over a precipice, I should not be too astonished if, at the time I have reached the bottom, I have broken something and am in pain. But this is not the kind of suffering that we are looking at here, the kind that results from our own sin or foolishness. Here in Job, we see a man who has lived as hard as he can to be blameless, to walk in all of God's ways, and to fulfil God's requirements. A man of whom God's judgment is that he is 'blameless and upright'.

In fact, not only did Job stay away from that precipice we just thought about, he also built a fence to keep others from hurting themselves, too. After his children had feasted and drunk, he would pray and offer sacrifices for them, saying, 'Perhaps my sons have sinned and cursed God in their hearts' (Job 1:5). His religion was not skin deep; 'Job did this continually' (same verse) - it was not just a one-off.

It is *that* kind of person suffering which is the real enigma, sometimes expressed in the phrase, 'Why do bad things happen to good people?' This is the question that plagues us whenever we see or experience first-hand the suffering of the innocent or the good. The question of suffering in general is difficult enough to understand, but it becomes a lot more acute when we see people suffering who do not deserve what happens to them. Where is the justice of God in these situations? How can he allow it? The book of Job is going to help us to come to some answers to these sorts of questions.

'God is Love' Under Attack

God is love (1 John 4:8, 16). This is the best one word definition of who God is that we can find. There is no greater way to talk about him. Moreover, God is revealed to us perfectly in Jesus, and his love—and therefore *who he is*, as he *is* love—is revealed to us perfectly as Jesus hangs on the cross and dies for us. Our God is a God who *gives himself* for us; a God who is perfect Love. As Jesus said, 'Greater love has no one than this, that one lay down his life' (John 15:13).

The fact that God is love, and that he runs the universe according to his love, is challenged by Satan at the outset of the book of Job. Whether love is the best way to run the universe or not is the question which keeps raising itself as we read the arguments of Job and his friends, and as we see the suffering with which Job is inflicted. It is the big challenge brought by Satan: is a 'God who is love' really fit to be in charge of the universe?

> *Does Job fear God for nothing? Have you not made a hedge about him and his house and all that he has on every side? You have blessed the work of his hands, and his possessions have increased in the land. But put forth your hand now and touch all that he has; he will surely curse you to your face. (Job 1:9-11)*

Here, Satan attacks God's leadership of love by saying that the kind of God who is revealed in Jesus on the cross, the God of love, is not worth serving. He argues that none of his creatures are capable of truly loving him. There is no such thing as pure, altruistic love in the created universe. Satan's proposal is that 'power' is the only language the universe understands and responds to. His philosophy of leadership could be summed up in the phrase 'Might is Right'.

Satan does not challenge the fact that God is love—he knows this to be true. His attack is to say that a God of love, who looks like Calvary, is not a fit sovereign for the universe. If we have a God, like God *is* in Christ, whom we see revealed on the Cross, then this sort of God is not adequate for running this universe he has created. 'A God of love is not the final answer to the problems and needs of this world' is the ubiquitous, whispered temptation of the Enemy.

But in spite of Satan's lies, the fact that God is love makes love supreme in the universe. Even atheists, at times, have reacted against the temptations of the Enemy and held love in first place. Bertrand Russell, the staunch atheist philosopher, is reported as saying (perhaps in an unguarded moment), 'Love is better than hate—but I cannot tell you why.' Though their definitions of love may be inadequate, many who do not know our God recognise the supremacy of love.

Unfortunately, many Christians do *not* recognise it. Though the Bible tells us that 'God is love', and that he is motivated by love ('God so *loved* the world that He gave His only begotten Son'), many Christians want to say, 'Ah, yes; but he is also 'almighty' or 'the judge' or 'the creator' or 'righteous'' and sometimes they make these attributes equally as important as love. God is indeed those things, but he is Love above all else. Before God was ever a creator, and therefore when he had no one to judge or rule or declare unrighteous, he existed Father, Son and Spirit in an eternal relationship of love. That means he is a *loving* judge, a *loving* creator, Almighty *Love*. Some Christians put God's power, his almightiness, before his love. If God's power, and no longer his love, is supreme, then we find ourselves with a God who controls everything, good and evil, that happens in his world. And that is the answer some Christians give to the problem of suffering. But it is not an answer that makes sense of God's love.

So, this is the question that troubles us all the way through the book of Job. Is God's love really the best way of running the universe, or is sheer power— the 'might is right' philosophy—really a better way to do it?

How Can God Be Both Loving And Almighty?

One of the most common questions we are asked as Christians must be: *why does a loving God allow suffering* in his world? I am sure that as you have tried to answer it, you have had to take into account these two factors: God's love and his almightiness. "If God is both loving *and* almighty, able to do absolutely anything, wouldn't he do something about my little girl who is ill in hospital? Wouldn't he do something about the tragic events that we read about in the papers? Wouldn't he intervene on behalf of starving and oppressed nations? Wouldn't he stop hurricanes and tidal waves in their tracks before they wreaked their havoc? If God is all-loving, and loves his people, if he is also all-*mighty*, surely almighty love would actually *act*? That is the tension concerning the problem of suffering and the justice of God. In the face of terrible suffering in the world, how can God be all-loving *and* almighty, at the same time?

Many people struggle with why God doesn't stop the suffering of the innocent, so much so that they eventually turn away from God altogether. The book of Revelation paints a beautiful vision of the future where God does just that. The fact that we do not experience that kind of perfect universe right now leads some to believe that either God *cannot*, or that he *will not*, stop the suffering and evil that exist.[1] He either *cannot*, because he is not almighty; or he *will not*, because he is not all-good, all-loving.[2]

---

1 There is of course the alternative, as found in certain Eastern philosophies, that suffering and evil do not really exist.

2 *That is the classical problem of what is known as *theodicy*, the justice of God: where is justice in the universe when the innocent suffer?*

However, as Christians, we believe our God is all-loving *and* all-powerful. How, then, do we explain the existence of suffering and evil in this world? There have been two main ways of addressing this, and they both revolve around the question of which comes *first* in God, which is primordial: his love, or his almightiness? Is God, in the base and essence of his being, love, or is he, at the heart of who he is, power? In other words, do we believe in 'God is love', or 'Might is right'?

'Might is Right'

Many of us, if we were honest, on careful analysis of ourselves and the kind of politics that we espouse, would have to say that we believe in the 'might is right' God – after all, 'might is right' gets things done. 'Might is right' does not allow things that are out of order to happen; it puts them down, finishes them off, affects an immediate change. Deep down, perhaps we feel that the wishy-washy sentimentalism of a God of love allows all kinds of things to go astray, with devastating results in the world today. We prefer a God who is primarily a God of power, the 'almighty' God, because he can run everything better! We would rather have the law and order of being slapped down if anybody gets out of line, the summary judgment, because then bad people are no longer able to continue with their evil and cause further pain.

We like that kind of thing—don't we? That is why we find it difficult when God does not step in and judge evil immediately. This is the other half of the problem of suffering; why doesn't the loving God use his power to stop suffering, and furthermore, why does he not judge there and then the people who are causing it? Neither seems to happen in the world we live in, and we sometimes feel confused or angry that God does not intervene and change situations in this way.

But you see, the 'might is right' God runs everything according to *his* will. No one else has any freedom. He uses his power, his might, to force everything and everyone to do exactly what he wants them to. If we worship a 'might is right' God, then we have to be prepared that he may not take our wishes into account as he intervenes (or not) in the world. If you have ever read the story by Albert Camus called *La Peste* ('The Plague'), you will see a parody of the 'might is right' God. In it, a plague carried by rats runs through a North African town, and the people are dying like flies. The humanist doctor, a man who does not believe in God, and the rat-catcher work together to stop the plague. The doctor deals with the pain in people's lives; the rat-catcher with the source of the problem: the rats that are carrying the disease. The priest, however, stands by and does nothing. He says that it is the will of God—after all, God made the rats, he made the disease, he made it such that human bodies can succumb to the disease, therefore 'the will of God be done.' The conclusion? God does nothing to help his people; we must abandon hope in him and look to one another to solve the problems of the world.

Camus' story is a devastating comment on this kind of quiescent, passive Christianity (although I'd rather call it 'Godianity' as it does not seem to have much to do with Christ or his teachings) that says that almighty God is running the whole thing anyway, so let's just stand by and watch it happen. It is a caricature, of course, but one that European Christianity deserves for the kind of thinking we have put over for many centuries. This is how many people understand Christianity, and why they abandoned it, especially after the horrors of two World Wars. It is also why many abandon it today after suffering personal tragedy. Christians have answered suffering with 'God is somehow working in all these things', and 'there is a much greater, more majestic, divine purpose behind (for example) letting that little girl die of typhoid, or the devastation left from war.' 'There is a great tapestry being woven,' it is said, 'and we can only see the back of it, the ugly side. It looks a mess; but one day we shall see the glorious picture on the front—the greater, divine purpose being worked out.' We say these things to preserve the 'might is right' God we think we are better off with, even though we cannot understand his actions. This view of God has almost achieved the backing of the authority of Scripture in some circles, but it is not a satisfactory answer to the problem of suffering. Nor is it a true one! And, most importantly, it is not a Bible one. Our God is not a God of 'the end justifies the means', who will sacrifice the lives of innocent children in order to achieve a higher purpose. I'm not sure how anybody can believe that after seeing and hearing Jesus. Nevertheless, we have sometimes been guilty of saying these kinds of things, albeit as gently as we can, to try and comfort those who have been bereaved, or who need some source of encouragement in their difficulty and their pain. 'It must be God's will, and so submit.'

As we have preached the gospel, we have often presented alongside it a view of God's management of this world and his relationship with it, which is not the Christian gospel. Thus, when someone suffers terribly and dies, we say that it was 'the will of God'; and so we contribute to the idea that *everything* that happens, down to the most minute detail, is ordered and ordained by God. I don't think Jesus was really into this idea, do you? Otherwise he would not have said, 'Pray, then, in this way: "…Your will be done"' (Matt. 6:9, 10). If God's will is being done all the time anyway, we do not need to pray that. Nor would he have encouraged and exhorted us to follow him, in loving our neighbours and enemies, if everything that happens is God's will—there would be no point, as whatever we did would be God's will.

Nevertheless, this idea is greatly comforting for many people in the West. It is very comforting for those of us who are 'at ease in Zion' (Amos 6:1); we feel maybe we are getting our deserts after all the privileges we have enjoyed. It can be also a comforting thought for people, after they have suffered, to look back and say they do not understand it, but that somehow God was ordaining all those things, so they must have been all right.

Though we have promulgated such ideas again and again in the history of the Christian church, this approach, in the final analysis, is not satisfactory. Our view of God, and of his relationship with this world, *has* to change if we are to give an adequate answer to the great mass of people who left the Christian church after the Great War. They left because they did not think that anyone could possibly suffer to the extent that they had suffered, and because their Christian faith was inadequate to meet that colossal challenge. To see your mates' skulls being eaten out by rats as they are left dead in the trenches—it was appalling for those who came back from the 1914-1918 war—and then to be told that it was God's will! They did not know how to recover from or account for it in the terms of their inherited (so-called) Christian faith. This was one of the major contributions to church decline in Europe.

It was then tipped over the balance by the Second World War. What was left (as it were) of European Christianity received the final blow, bringing unbelief and a complete disregard of the church. The church was counted as irrelevant, because of the inability of Christianity to answer the challenge of what was happening to people. As a result, that generation did not bother to teach the gospel to their children, and we now have masses of people who do not even know what the gospel is. These questions about God and suffering have contributed to the process of church decline, particularly in Europe.

As Christians, we need to recover some biblical, Jesus-like answers to the problem of suffering that do not resort to a 'might is right' God to make sense of it all. How does the 'God who is love' deal with evil in his world? How does he reconcile his promise of salvation with his apparent inaction in the atrocities we face day to day in life? How is he going to handle the problem of suffering, so that it is finished with forever?

2

God is Love

The book of Job is going to help us to reconcile the God of love
with the God of power, without adopting a 'might is right' attitude. Although the word 'love' is only once used in the whole
book (and it is not in the context of loving God)[1] we also find
the word 'worship'. Job's response to the first set of disasters is
that he 'fell to the ground and worshiped' (Job 1:20). To worship
is to love. The Hebrew word here literally means to bow oneself
down. It is a kind of 'love-making' to God, an extreme admira-
tion and abandon of oneself utterly to the will and pleasure of the
other. Worship is giving oneself to another. Our worship to God
expresses our devotion to him, our adoration of him, the wonder
of belonging to him, the wonders of who he is. God wants us to
love him, and to love one another. Jesus tells us that these are the

---

1 Job 19:19; Job says, 'All my associates abhor me, And those I love
   have turned against me.'

two greatest commandments God gave us: '"...you shall love the Lord your God with all your heart, and with all your soul, and with all your mind, and with all your strength" ... "You shall love your neighbour as yourself." There is no other commandment greater than these.' (Mk. 12:30, 31; see also Matt. 22:36-40).

Free will

The problem with love unfolds like this: in order for us to be able to love God and to love one another, as Jesus commanded, God has given us free will. You cannot compel or force real love. If I stand threateningly over my wife and beat her on the head, or slap her round the face, saying, 'Come on, love me!' I don't think you would say we've got very much going for our marriage. It would probably be divorce in the morning! Love is something that cannot be coerced; if it were to be, it would not be love. Love must be the voluntary giving of one to the other. That is the kind of loving that God is giving us when he gives *himself* to us. That is also the kind of loving that we are here to give to him, and to one another, in order that the love of God may permeate the church of Christ. So Jesus says, 'By this all men will know that you are My disciples, if you have love for one another' (John 13:35). What does that love look like? 'Love one another, even as I have loved you, that you also love one another' (John13:34). This can mean two things and probably both are intended. First, we should love each other in the same way, degree and intensity as Jesus loved us; the love that took him to the Cross for us. Second, because we have been loved by Jesus, we can, out of that relationship and in His love, find the grace and persistence to love one another. That is the sort of wonderful Kingdom life that the Lord has in his heart for us to enjoy.

We might well wonder why God has given his creatures free

will when they so often use it for wrong. But without free will, we could neither choose to love, nor to do right, and therefore we could not enjoy the true goodness, joy and happiness that God's Kingdom promises. A universe where everyone lives like a robot operated at the will of the Creator by remote control would hardly be worth making. The book of Job shows us something about how this free will universe functions; we see Satan exerting his will, going around randomly, as it were, 'roaming about on the earth and walking around on it' (Job 1:7); we see Job using his will to choose to keep worshipping God, even when everything in his life was falling apart. That un-coerced choice is at the very heart of love (Job 1:20), and it is through this lens that we will begin to open up the book of Job and start to understand some deep truths about how God has decided to run his universe.

Biblical or Philosophical Terms?

Part of the problem of understanding how God can allow suffering stems from the fact that as Christians we have adopted a false dichotomy between the concepts of 'love' and 'power'; we think we have to choose between two contradictory alternatives that are not really even on the same map. Using *biblical* terminology, we assert that 'God is love', but using a Latin *philosophical* term, we accept that God is also 'omnipotent'. Yet logically and experientially it seems that never the twain shall meet.

If we look at the problem again, however, just using biblical terms, we find that the Bible tells us that 'God is love' (1 John 4:8, 16), and it also tells us that he is 'the Almighty' (e.g. Rev. 1:8)[2]. The word for 'almighty' in Greek is '*pantokrator*'. It is made up

---

2 It is worth noting that the word 'almighty' is always used as a title (or name) for God, whereas 'Love' is not his title; it is who God is—in his essence.

of two parts: '*panto-*' from '*pas*', meaning 'all'; and '*kratos*', which means 'might', 'force', 'strength', or 'power'. So, God is *all-mighty*, *panto-krator*, all power, strength and might belongs ultimately to him.

This is very different from saying that God is 'omnipotent' – this term is made up of two Latin words: '*omni-*' meaning 'all' and '*potens*' from the verb 'to be able'. To be omnipotent implies that God can do everything and anything he likes. The Bible uses the term 'almighty'.

Moreover, as we have seen, this almighty God has delegated some of his all-power in the form of free will. He has given us a very limited, but still real, power to choose. It is limited in the sense that we cannot choose to do *anything* we want: we do not have *that* much power! I cannot, for example, choose to flap my arms and fly off. But Paul understands his free will when he says, for instance, 'to will is present with me' (Rom. 7:18, KJV). The devil also was given some 'power'. He had 'the power ['*kratos*', in the Greek] of death' (Heb. 2:14). It was delegated to him by God. In fact, C. S. Lewis suggested rather quaintly that being the Lord's Chief Executioner was the thing that went to Satan's head and caused him to think he was God himself. Perhaps he thought he had the power to take life whenever he wanted.

The fact that the power was delegated to Satan shows too, of course, that the devil is not almighty—nothing can be almighty except the one who gives out the 'might'. The Christian worldview is not a dualism as in, for example, Zoroastrianism, where there is a dark force and a light force, equal and opposite, that are locked in an eternal battle with each other. In that system, you cannot say which is the better one: they both just 'are'. Neither comes first, good does not come before evil, nor love before hate—they just are love and hate. Only Christianity, however, says that there is good and evil in the world, love and hate, but that love is supreme, love comes first, because love is from God: God is love.

Of course, God is the only one called '*panto*-krator', *all*-powerful, *al*mighty. All power, all might, comes from him, is delegated from him, and ultimately belongs to him. We would not have any power, any ability to choose, unless he had given it to us. His will is that we should have wills, real wills that can disobey or obey. Thus, if we do something wrong, it is both *against* his will (he did not want us to do it), and *within* his will (he wanted us to have the power to choose). He keeps this universe running, moment by moment. He could pull the plug whenever he wanted. He keeps every bit of power running, including our power to choose, even when we use it to do something he does not want us to. That is what it means that God is Almighty, and he is Love: Almighty Love.

We might expect God to sovereignly remove the power to choose from someone who is about to choose to harm somebody else. But if he took back that power, he would not have really given it in the first place. The only way to give free will is to let people keep it. If you always take it back when they do not do what you want them to, then you have not really given them free will. They would only be free to 'choose' when they chose what you wanted; in other words, they could not choose what they wanted; they would not be free. Thus, God's delegation of power has made a universe that can go wrong—to an extent—as well as go right. We have the power to choose to do evil things, and sometimes we choose to do them. God does not want this to happen, but only a pretty strange and unloving 'god' would make a perfect universe in the beginning, and then 'will' all kinds of evil things to happen in it. It is philosophically impossible for God to give us free will and at the same time to determine everything that we do with it.

This is not to say that the future is totally open, outside of God's control and that anything can happen. God's will, our wills, angelic and demonic wills all exist in the mix. They may well, to some extent, all be competing, but it is not much of a competition when you put a beginner at chess against a grand-master, to use an analogy. We all know who is going to win. God is still in charge of our universe, despite the battle of wills that rages within it. When he says he is going to come back and wrap the whole thing up, defeating evil once and for all, he will!

Goldingay in his commentary on Daniel uses a dramatic analogy of the same concept. Instead of the chess grand-master, God is like the governor of a prison in which a riot has erupted. The governor and his prison staff confine and limit the wills of the angry prisoners, but of course they do not fully control their individual actions until overall order is ultimately restored.

Loving Means Limiting Yourself for the Other

God is presented in the Bible as a God of love; thus he is not a God who can do anything and everything whenever He likes—and we do not always like that! We want to hang onto the fact that God can do anything. We even sing songs about it. But the amazing truth is that God has limited himself on our behalf. The Bible itself tells us that there are some things God can't do. He cannot lie, for example (Tit. 1:2; Heb. 6:18). He cannot be tempted (Jas. 1:13). Reason tells us, as we have seen, that God cannot force anyone to love him freely, and indeed the Bible never shows him compelling anyone to love him, but rather he gives freedom to those who choose to reject him, whilst all the time reaching out to them in love (cf Jesus and Judas in John 13).

To give another, more trivial example: a farmer might pray for rain for his wilting crops in the hot summer, whilst at the same time you and I, planning our holiday, are praying for it *not* to rain. God simply *cannot* grant both requests. Two prayers like that, multiplied by six billion people on the earth, cause a colossally complex problem to the Almighty God. How can he run this universe making sure everybody gets what they want all the time? He can't because that is not the way he made it. There are certain limits on how things exist and interact together. In some ways, it would make life a lot easier for God if he *could* make it rain and be dry in the same spot at the same time. Then all the conflicting prayer requests we send up to him could be answered at the same time, and everybody would be happy! But that wouldn't be the universe God chose to create.

Some Jewish rabbis recognised that simply by creating the universe at all, God chose to limit himself to some extent. If God has made something, he has *not* made the alternative. That is a limitation, in a strict, logical sense. If that is the kind of God we have — a God who limits himself on our behalf — then we have the kind of God who *can* have a relationship with us. There can be no relationship unless there is an ability to give and receive. It would be a pretty poor marriage if one partner was able to dominate 100% and the other was 100% passive. If God relates to us like that then we are living in a puppet show universe. Relationship means giving and receiving, and that requires both parties to limit themselves at times.

If you love somebody, you limit yourself on their behalf; you do not force your own way upon them entirely. God is love, so he is rather used to this limiting stuff — which may sound quite contrary to certain popular Christian beliefs! But this is the God of the Bible. He *is* almighty: if he wanted to, he could at this moment pull the plug on everything, so that the universe went out, like a TV being switched off. All power belongs to him. But God has created something that has a realm of relationships requiring love and free will, and so he will not just step in and take it away when the going gets tough, but he allows it to go on operating in order that true relationships can be established. That is the God who is behind the book of Job.

The Pre-Eminence of Love

The pre-eminence of love is at the heart of the Christian message, if not, in one sense, the whole of our message. *God is love*; we cannot get any deeper than that. We saw that love is no love which is forced, or which forces. That should be right out of the Christian picture. Forcing people to do something instead of loving them only produces a reaction of violence or hostility. That is why the history of the church with its wars and crusades is so deplorable. The love of God as seen in Christ on the cross must have the pre-eminence in all of our thinking as Christians. It should colour every other doctrine of the New Testament and of the Old. The book of Job begins to reveal to us that behind the scenes a battle rages over which is the more important, which is supreme, which has the pre-eminence — a battle, in fact, about who God *is* — is he sheer power, or is he love like Calvary, that is, Almighty Love?

Although it might at times seem attractive, we cannot allow ourselves to adopt the 'might is right' doctrine. If we truly think that God is sheer power at the heart of who he is, then we will all end up getting on his side quick-smart, spiritual sycophants who are looking after our own interests by buttering up a God who is likely to put us down if we do not join up with him (e.g. Is. 29:13).

The universe is only understandable by revelation. God's revelation of himself to us emphasizes his love as seen in Christ. 'For God so loved the world that he gave…' (John 3:16). This is the great *action* of love; love is not just being, it is acting. And the divine act of love was to give his Son. The revelation of God is brought to its culmination and conclusion on the cross. That is the kind of government of the universe that we as Christians should want to stand by. That is the kind of kingdom that will last forever. If we build a kingdom upon 'might is right', then might will provoke a reaction which brings yet more hostility and violence. We sow violence and we reap violence, so we sow more violence and we reap more violence, and there is no conclusion to the unending hell of this situation.

The only way to build a universe, the only way to have a kingdom which will reign forever and ever, is if we build it by *our own* blood, not somebody else's; and ultimately God builds it by his own blood (Acts 20:28): the blood of Jesus.

'God is love' or 'might is right'? That is the battle that lies behind the scenes of this universe, in which we become engaged and involved when we become Christians. We are either contributing to one scheme or the other. Job was being called to stand for the truth that 'God is love' — in a unique and special way which we shall analyse as we look deeper into the book.

3

Love is Attacked

And the Lord said to Satan, 'Have you considered My servant Job? For there is no one like him on the earth, a blameless and upright man, fearing God and turning away from evil.'

Then Satan answered the Lord, 'Does Job fear God for nothing? Have You not made a hedge about him and his house and all that he has, on every side? You have blessed the work of his hands, and his possessions have increased in the land. But put forth Your hand now and touch all that he has; he will surely curse You to Your face.'

Then the Lord said to Satan, 'Behold, all that he has is in your power, only do not put forth your hand on him.'

So Satan departed from the presence of the Lord. (Job 1:8-12)

You could almost say that God starts all the trouble here in these verses. He is so *thrilled* about Job—can you believe it? God is delighted when he finds somebody who is blameless and upright! This does not mean that Job had never sinned; but when he did, he *repented*, literally the word means he 'turned away' from sin. He gets right with God again. He is 'blameless and upright', and God is pleased with him.

Later there came a day when God's own Son was being baptised. The Father looked down upon him and he was thrilled! 'Look!' he said, 'That's my Son—that's my boy!' He was so overjoyed that it is almost as though he fell down out of heaven upon Jesus, in the shape of the Holy Spirit. God had long been looking for a true human on whom he could pour out his Spirit. He was looking for humankind to start living up to the destiny for which he had created it. When he found true humanity in Jesus, his heart leapt with great euphoria, 'Oh, wonderful! That's my Son, that's my child. That is the sort of human being I wanted!' His Spirit was poured forth so that the rest of us could now walk in that same destiny intended for human-kind and be conformed to the image of his Son.

2,000 years before Jesus came, God saw Job and he was excited, because he saw in him some of that righteousness and blamelessness he was looking for. Perhaps you and I tend to think, 'Well, there are six billion of us anyway. Who cares whether somebody is a bit more righteous than somebody else?' But we are not the God of love, searching throughout the history of humanity for someone through whom to right the wrongs of a sinful world. God does care about righteousness! His whole plan and destiny for humankind depends upon it. And in Job, we have a biblical revelation of a God who loves his world, who is looking for the best in the world, and who wants us to experience the best in it because he loves us.

Satan's Challenge

Satan sees that God is excited about Job and is determined to spoil it. But God will not contain his joy and delight in Job just because of Satan. It is not right for God to hide the truth, or be something he is not, out of fear of what the Enemy might do. Satan knew about Job because of God's openness and integrity. He uses this information to challenge God's character: 'You like Job, don't you, God? You think he's upright and blameless? Well, no wonder, look how much he gets out of his relationship with you! Nice family, plenty of money, property, sheep and cattle. It's not surprising he worships you, is it?"

This is the kind of Christianity that some of us have been reared in: if you obey God, you generally have a good time, if you disobey him, you may have a rough time. If things are going badly for you, you must be doing something wrong. There is some truth in this, of course. If we live in God's world the way he made us to live in it, things will mostly work the way they should, and we shall be blessed, (unless Satan decides to launch an attack on us). But Satan is accusing Job of only serving God because of the benefits he receives. His love is "cupboard love". Does he fear God for *nothing*?

Satan's challenge strikes at the very heart of who God is and how he made his universe to be: Job doesn't love God *because he is almighty love*, he has to be getting something out of it. Satan claims that altruistic love, selfless love, does not exist in the universe and is not valued amongst God's creatures. 'Calvary love' — love with no strings attached — is an unreality, God's pipe-dream. Thus there is no such thing as pure worship in the universe, nothing worth God getting excited over. This is the heart of the cosmic battle that forms the backdrop to the narrative of the story of Job.

God's Response

What can God do to come back at this?

> *'Then the LORD said to Satan, "Get out of here, you're a liar, and a murderer from the beginning!" (Slap, slap!)'*

Did he say that? No. That is what we might like him to say, because in our hearts we are tempted to believe in Satan's philosophy. We wish God would have got hold of Satan and given him a good beating, or a clip round the ear (or whatever the equivalent is in the heavenly council of God). After all, God is bigger and more powerful than Satan. He should have thrown him out and said, 'I will *not* have that kind of behaviour in my kingdom!', shouldn't he?

Had God done that, however, Satan would have suffered a spiritual black eye, or bruised ear, but he also would have crept out of God's presence with a great sneer on his face. Everybody in the council room, including God, would have known that Satan had really won. He could rejoice in the knowledge that God really believed in exactly the same philosophy as he did. Might is right. Almighty Love doesn't really exist. In the end, God has to resort to Satan's kingdom to get his will done, and because he's the biggest, he can slap Satan down.

Many of us as Christians want a God like that. We even want that kind of leadership in the church at times. This was true even in the New Testament church. Paul found that Corinth preferred the leadership style of false apostles. They 'slap you in the face', he says, 'and you put up with them.' The Corinthians even called them 'the super-apostles'! They loved this kind of leadership: flashy, bossy, belligerent[1].

---

1   See 2 Cor. 11:19-21, and also 1 Cor. 4:1-13.

However, God's servants do not look like this. Paul (possibly a nickname meaning 'tiny') was traditionally thought to be bow-legged, short and not particularly attractive. Jesus was a 'root out of parched ground' with 'no stately form or majesty…nor appearance that we should be attracted to him' (Is. 53:2). Paul was being dismissed and overlooked by the Corinthians, while the 'super-apostles' would demand things from people and then put them down. 'I need your tithes; pay up!' *slap, slap*—they existed in the first century, and some of them are still around today. Though many Christians like their leaders to be flashy and powerful and in control of the situation, it does not really solve any internal problems; it does not give priority to love and relationship.

That is why God does not simply beat Satan into submission. This is a fundamental truth about God's character: *God cannot behave and act in the way that the Devil does, competing power with power.* He competes power with love. He demonstrates that he has a better way, ultimately the way of the cross.

Does Pure, Altruistic Love Exist?

Satan would have us all believe that altruistic love doesn't exist. That all love is selfish in this universe and that, contrary to what God says, we should all live accordingly. That is the war that lies behind the universe. That is the war that we are engaged in every time we are tempted, as Job was, to curse God, or to curse the situations around us, and to say that such a love does not exist, even in the heart of God. That is the war that we give into when we are not prepared to give love back to God, or other people, unless they first give us something we want.

Satan's challenge is an indictment against both God and man. God is not worth loving and serving for who he is in himself, only for what you can get out of him. Human beings are not capable of pure, altruistic love, only selfishness.

Let me make it more poignant, for a moment. Imagine a man whose wife is dying with cancer. He sits with her in the hospital and holds her hand. He goes through the pain with her, constantly at her bedside; in fact, sometimes he feels more pain in his soul than she does in her body because of the agony of losing her, and the fact that she is going through something that he cannot change or do anything about. He gets absolutely nothing out of his wife except pain. She does not wash his clothes or cook him dinner (it is an old-fashioned family!); she cannot give him any cuddles. He gets nothing back for all he puts in. You would say that man *loved* his wife. People show that kind of devotion across the world every day. Surely we can't agree with the Devil's assessment of human love!

On the other hand, imagine the same man as he pushes off to play fast and loose with the woman next door, saying, 'well, my wife gives me nothing now—what do *I* get out of this relationship…?' It is all too familiar a story in 'romantic' films or books today. We have replaced real love with a 'romantic' substitute, and we have lost the philosophy that comes from God; that Almighty Love sits on the throne of the universe, and Almighty Love is prepared to go through these kinds of experiences for the sake of the ones he loves. The second story may have a romantic happy ending where he marries someone new and lives happily ever after. We may be open-minded, sociologically developed, or politically correct, and say, 'Well, he had to have his emotional and sexual fulfilment from somewhere'. But ultimately we would not honestly say that the man *loved* his wife as he left her. No one would say that to abandon one's pain-filled spouse, dying alone in agony would be the way that love is expressed. Love is expressed in empathy, in identification, in sharing the experiences of the other one; going down the road to death as far as you possibly can and standing at the doorway until the final goodbye is said.

The person is intrinsically worth it in themselves, whether you get anything out of them or not; that is what love believes. That is what love is like.

If there is not some point in this life where we get nothing out of our obedience to God, where our service to him seems to bring no rewards, then maybe we shouldn't be counting ourselves so blessed; maybe God has never seen fit to lead us into a situation like the one in which Job found himself; maybe, unlike Job, when God looks at our hearts he is not sure that our response to suffering would reflect *his* heart. Would our actions justify *him* to the rest of the universe? Would we demonstrate that Almighty Love *is* the only final answer for its salvation? Every time we choose to worship God, in the bad times as much as the good, we are proving that Almighty Love is the only thing that makes sense of our pain and our tears, of our laughter and our joys, of our relationships and all the things that go on in our human experience. We are proving that to love is what we were created to live for. If Almighty Love is the God who lies behind the universe, then he made us with the capacity to love with everything that we are, whether we get anything out of it or not. If we then choose only to love somebody for what we get out of them, we have sold ourselves short of Calvary Love. We have experienced only a shadow of the fullness of the love that we can taste in this life – no wonder some of us think the world is such a cold and colourless place! But Job begins to demonstrate Calvary Love for us; that is where his story will take us, as we read on.

Of course, Job did not fully know that this was what was happening behind the scenes of his life. However, when we face this kind of battle, we have an advantage over him, we have an insight into 'behind the scenes'. We have not only read about Satan's challenge in the first two chapters of Job, but we have seen God's answer to it walked out in our Lord Jesus Christ. We have seen him cry out on the cross: 'My God, My God, *why* have You forsaken me?' In that moment, the perfect life Jesus had lived in service of and devotion to his Father in heaven afforded him no comfort. He knew what it is to love God and get *absolutely nothing out of it* except pain, agony, distress, torment: hell itself. Yet in that place he still went on loving and trusting: 'Father, into Your hands I commit my Spirit' (Luke 23:46). And it is in that place that we see the final triumph of this battle, the final defeat of Satan's challenge to altruistic love. Moreover, that victory is being worked out today, day in and day out, through the devotion and worship of his Body, the Church.

The Cause Is In Us

> *Does Job fear God for nothing? (Job 1:9)*

> *...although you incited Me against him, to ruin him without cause... (Job 3:2)*

'For nothing' and 'without cause' in these verses are exactly the same Hebrew word[2]. You may remember Jesus saying something similar, 'they hated Me without a cause' (John 15:25).

Some people try to find a cause for everything. There has to be a cause why this particular person is a mugger or a murderer, there must be a cause why this one is twisted up in his sexuality and destroys young children; perhaps we can find the cause in his childhood experiences or in his current circumstances. These factors undoubtedly contribute to the formation of a person's character and will influence the choices they make. But ultimately—that is, when all environmental conditioning or detrimental experiences are recognised, identified and allowed for—there is *no external*

---

2   The word is chinnam.

cause that makes us choose to be the person we are. Rationalism is always looking for a cause and effect relationship; it is based on an empirical system that says every action has an equal and opposite reaction, the effects we see around us have equivalent causes. Perhaps we like this system because it reduces individual responsibility for ones choices and actions. But ultimately, God holds no one else accountable for the things we do with our lives. *The cause for our actions is found in the choices we make; the cause is within you, within me, within demons, within angels, within Satan and within God himself.*

Christian thinking has often been unwilling to accept this level of responsibility, worrying that it somehow takes away from God's control of his creation. It has led to a cause-effect world-view where God is the ultimate cause of everything, the starting point for every chain of events. Secular thinking may have taken God out of the picture, but it has hung onto the cause-effect chains, thus perpetrating a sociological disaster whereby everything a person does is a result of a past experience. This person is a murderer, but it's not really his fault, because his Grandmother used to beat him when he was a child. But how do you ever call anyone to account in this system? How do we shape a society of different people living together when it is impossible to expect anyone to be able to conform to or abide by any standards of behaviour? We need to accept that the fundamental cause for behaviour is *ourselves*. Of course, once we have started down the pathway of a bad decision, we may be helped on the way by circumstances or past experience; but the ultimate cause is within the human being. Two people, twins even, can be brought up and treated in exactly the same way, and yet the final product of their lives will be immensely different. Biology and environmental factors only contribute so much to a person – but the whole is determined by the choices that take place inside of us, how we decide to react to the good and the bad done to us. Of course, our choices eventually lead to us being enslaved to sin, as Romans 7:14 reminds us. But even in this passage, when Paul declares his inability to *do* good, he also insists in contrast that he still has the *will* to do it[3].

The truth is, Christian thinking has to accept that the cause is in us. God has no right to judge the human race, or you and me individually, unless the cause for the actions for which we are being judged is found somewhere within you and me. If the cause is not us, then whoever else caused it would be to blame. A fair judge will be able to peel off contributing factors en route - the bad childhood, the traumatic experience - but ultimately it is my own response to the things that are happening, my own choices, my own will, that brings me legitimately into God's judgment.

I believe in human free will; I believe it enables us as human beings to repent and ultimately to live differently by God's grace. If we do not accept that we have a will which can make choices, we cannot say, as Nathan the prophet did to David, 'You are the man!'[4] Unless I can point the finger at myself, or receive somebody else's pointing finger, in order to accept my responsibility in the things that have been done, I will never see change in my life. Nor will I be equipped to affect change in the world around me when things are going wrong. When I stand up and say, '*I* am the man; I am the one who did this, and I need God's help to change', then I begin to find answers in my life from him. That is when I become a *real human being*, instead of a bit of putty, or a wet flannel that flaps around, or a Charlie Brown that always sits

---

3 Romans 7:18.

4 I.e. '*You* did it—it's *your* fault!' See the story of David's sin with Bathsheba in 2 Samuel 11 and 12 (verse quoted - 12:7).

on the fence and never makes up his mind about anything. The less we believe in human free will, the less able we are to call anything right or wrong, and the less able we are to stand up for anything positive in a world of confusing shades of grey. May God save us from society's disempowering worldview that sends us all into the hell of our own experience with no way out, rather than raising us up as human beings who choose to look the world in the face and say, 'I may be the only person who believes this, but I am going to live by it and die by it.' That is the calling that Jesus has for the human being. It offers a dignity that belongs to godlikeness - for these are the choices that God makes.

Since the beginning of humanity, our theology and philosophy has been trying to remove the responsibility of the human being to rise up and live in the dignity of being made in the image of God. On the first pages of the Bible, we find human beings trying to pass the buck[5]. Instead of blaming everybody else—'the serpent made me', or 'the woman *you gave me* made me'—we need to start saying, 'I am the man: I did it.' We need to stand up and play the man, play the woman. This is exactly what God says to Job at the end of his story, 'Stand on your feet, Job; gird up your loins. I want to speak to you.'[6] Man to man, as it were! God is treating the human being with the dignity of being human, expecting him to stand up and speak for himself, not crawl around on all fours whimpering like an animal.

To be human is not to be a mere lump of putty that has been moulded and conditioned by thousands of years of evolution, and has finally taken on the shape of you and me. Nor is it to be pas-

---

5   Genesis 3:11-13; note that the man tries to shift the blame not just
    to the woman, but also to God: 'The woman *You* gave to be with
    me…'

6   See Job 38:3, and 40:7.

sive because 'everything is ordained by God, all happening just as he has arranged it, I don't need to make an effort, it will all just happen without me.' It is a matter of standing up before God, in his light, and saying, 'God, help me. I want to choose to do what is right. I want to be one of those who follow in the footsteps of Jesus.' I hope you are beginning to see the idea, and to be inspired by it, as I am. Human free will lies at the heart of the issue of suffering and our response to it. Because we are made in God's image, we have a responsibility to act like he does when troubles come upon us, and in so doing we will have an incredibly positive impact into this suffering world.

4

The Heavenly Council

Reality Behind Picture-Language

> *Now there was a day when the sons of God came to pre-sent themselves before the Lord, and Satan also came among them. And the Lord said to Satan, 'From where do you come?' Then Satan answered the Lord and said, 'From roaming about on the earth and walking around on it.' (Job 1:6-7)*

In chapters 1 and 2 of Job, we see what we might call the 'super-natural backdrop to the universe'. We get to see behind the scenes of what is going on in the world we live in. Here in the book of Job, it is presented to us in terms of what appears to be a council, the Council of God. Of course, it is a picture; but a picture which tells us something about reality, nonetheless. It represents something real, just as when Jesus gives us a parable. Sometimes the Bible depicts the spiritual world in terms of a battle - Michael and his archangels fighting against the devil and his powers[1]. Sometimes it is a law court scene, and Satan, (whose name means 'the accuser'), is the prosecutor [2]. Picture language should not be dismissed as childish. We have no other way to talk about the supernatural mechanics of this wonderfully complex universe in which we live. We do the same thing in science, when we use pictures of 'currents' to talk about electricity - of course electricity does not literally flow like a river. In order to be able to understand, talk about and even interact with the unseen things, we need to think of them in concrete terms.

Job is a book for all times, all cultures, and all places. That is why it uses such vivid and easy-to-understand picture language. Job helps us to understand the sometimes conflicting experiences we have in the world, where we can feel God's love and power, yet still experience suffering, by painting us a picture of some kind of supernatural council. God communicates with the spiritual forces that lie behind the physical world, and brings them to account - they are answerable to him. These forces have different names in the Bible: 'principalities and powers'[3], 'mights and dominions'[4], 'thrones'[5], 'gods, sons of the Most High'[6], 'hosts of spiritual wickedness in the heavenly places'[7], 'the myriad company of the angels'[8], and many more. All these terms create pictures

---

1   See Daniel 10 and Rev 12:7
2   See 1 Tim 3:6 and Rev 12:10
3   Titus 3:1
4   Ephesians 1:21
5   Colossians 1:16
6   Psalm 82:6
7   Ephesians 6:12
8   Hebrews 12:22

for us to understand something real that lies behind the physical world.

The divinely inspired editor of the opening scenes of the book of Job shows us something of which Job himself was probably unaware. There is a spiritual battle going on behind the scenes of the world of which he is a part; but he does not fully understand it. The battle is over whether or not Almighty Love is fit to run the universe. Satan's challenge is issued in this committee or council context, which serves as a model for us to understand how God has delegated his power. We can begin to see it like an earthly 'cabinet meeting', where different people hold different delegated responsibilities, together with different views and opinions on how they should be carried out. They are gathered before the Almighty, who is, of course, Chair. He holds the ultimate responsibility for the universe, and he has to deal with all the interactions between those to whom he has delegated power. The biblical pictures of a committee (as portrayed here in Job), or a battleground, or a law court are attempts to describe how he handles those interactions. The point is: there is accountability and communication between God and his universe.

The battlefield picture explains why people suffer randomly – there are inevitably casualties of war, and we should not look at them as personal attacks. The law court picture shows us why individuals may suffer justly; our actions may be penalised for their consequences. There are winners and losers in a law suit, and sometimes we are made to pay, even for mistakes. But Job's picture of the heavenly council begins to unpack for us the subject of theodicy, God's justice. How and why does a just God allow his innocent people to suffer at the hands of wickedness?

What Is Reality?

At the heart of all the philosophical systems, all the thinking about this world of the last 400 years, lies the question: 'What *is* reality?' All sorts of answers have been offered. They each have something useful to contribute, but none can satisfactorily tell us *what reality is*.

Rationalism – I think therefore I am

Rationalism gave us 'I think, therefore I am'[9], but left us inside our heads, *thinking* about things, in a kind of abstract world of 'pure, rational thought'.

Empiricism – I observe therefore I am

That was not quite good enough, so along came Empiricism, which said that reality lay in what could be *weighed and measured*: in effect, what we can see or touch. But then we realised that our senses themselves can be affected by things; different people may see things from different points of view. Therefore, what is 'out there' under observation may not be the same as what is 'in here', in my mind.

Romanticism – I feel therefore I am

So, the Romanticists reacted to all this weighing and measuring by saying that reality is the *impact* that the world has on our *feelings*. It is not so much the things themselves, whether they can be weighed and measured or not, it is how we are *affected* by those things. But then we come up against the problem that there is no benchmark to say that love is better than hate—they are both just 'feelings' which are equally valid, equally 'reality'. If happiness

---

9   Descartes' "Discourse on Method"

is my benchmark, then I measure things by that and live by that. If what makes me happy makes someone else sad, there is no external reference to decide who is right and who is wrong. We fight it out for ourselves in a sea of emotions.

Existentialism – I choose therefore I am

Unhappy with this state of affairs, the Existentialists said that in actual fact, reality, or meaning, is what you choose it to be. Every individual creates his own reality internally, no system or evaluation can be imposed upon it from the outside. But the problem with this occurs again in how we judge what is a right choice and what is a wrong one. There is no standard given; if somebody chooses to be an oppressive dictator, how can we say it is wrong? And if we can't comment on, or intrude into one another's reality, then what relation does one human being's existence have with another?

Post-Modernism – I am not sure what I am!

Out of the Existentialist movement, more recently, post-modernism has arisen, which boldly asserts that there is nothing to measure anything by. There is no ultimate reality, everything is virtual. The problem of relating meaningfully to other human beings becomes irrelevant since the virtual reality can replace the physical reality. You can create sexual stimulus by looking at images or interacting with a computer screen; the feelings of hatred, sympathy, affection or revulsion feel just the same when you watch a film or a soap opera as when you relate to someone in real life. It is all *virtual* reality.

While there are truths to be discovered in all of these systems, none has managed to deal adequately and finally with the question. Thus, today we have reached the place where most people have abandoned the search for truth and reality, accepting that ultimately there is nothing behind anything.

Pulling Back the Veil

What we have here in the first chapters of the Book of Job is a pulling back of the veil over what is ultimately behind the universe, over what truth or reality is, *and it comes to us by revelation from God.* Wittgenstein was not wrong when he said that if there was any meaning to anything that happens in the universe, the meaning must come in from *outside* the universe where it is all happening[10]. The explanation must enter the system of the universe from elsewhere, otherwise it is simply a part of what needs to be understood in the first place. The revelation of God, breaking into our world, is therefore essential for ultimately laying hold of the truth of *what is.*

The eternal reality of God enters into this small bit of temporal, created energy and matter we call the earth *by revelation.* The explanation of Job's story is put in and unveiled by God for us in the first chapter. Job himself could not see it until God unveiled things directly to him, as we see at the close of the book. What is revealed to us is something of the reality of the way that God runs the world. It shows us a God who is excited when he sees a righteous and blameless person: a God who loves the world and is looking for the *best* in it; a God who wants us to experience the best, which is love, because he loves us.

The Council of God

The council of God in the heavens demonstrates the kind of *freedom* that exists within true loving. God does not just do the whole job of governing the universe by himself, like a kind of

---

10 Wittgenstein's "Notebooks"

lone ranger. Job introduces us to the supernatural realm on 'a certain day' when 'the sons of God presented themselves, and Satan amongst them'[11]—a very concrete picture of a committee in progress, which emphasises that *God is not running the show on his own.* Love never wants to do that, does it? It always wants to share. Loving is giving, and giving is loving - it is all the same thing in the end. God wants to run this world *together.*

In the heavenly realm, to help him in the government, there is a kind of spiritual, supernatural committee, to which *we* now have access by the Holy Spirit. We can put our vote in around the table! This may sound a bit of a trivial, earthly sort of picture, but it does express the corporate way in which God is *sharing government,* as he shares so much else with us. The supernatural beings which are in part responsible for the administration of this universe, holding it and gluing it together, are the 'principalities and the powers' of the New Testament, the 'gods' or 'sons of God' of Psalm 82, or the 'Prince of Greece' and the 'Prince of Persia' of Daniel 10; the Lord gathers this conglomerate of people, or 'powers', together with us and our prayers, in the day to day administration of the universe.

How God Governs Through His Council

God is not doing everything on his own—he has made creatures and he wants to share things with them. He shares his authority; he shares his administration, his ability to communicate and interact, to do things together. The heavenly council picture helps us to see that it is not simply God who calls all the shots. He is indeed the Chairman of the whole happening, but he lets other people's opinions come into the scene. When the devil sees evil things in the hearts of men and women, he has ground for operation there, which God does not take away.

---

11 Job 1:6

There are certain areas of the universe committed to the charge of these powers, and they are responsible to God for these areas. Psalm 82 portrays this for us clearly. We see God calling his rulers to account for judging unjustly and showing partiality to the wicked[12]. The book of Daniel shows us the principality of Persia and the principality of Greece in contention with each other[13]; they both have their claims around the throne of God. In the book of Kings[14], the council of God appears again, this time in a vision to Micaiah the prophet. God is looking to cause Ahab to fall; he does not do it himself, but looks for one of his council to come up with a plan. Different ideas are put forward until one 'spirit of deception' steps up and says, 'I will be a deceiving spirit in the mouth of all the prophets', and God releases him to do it. God does not exactly want deception to go forth. But the spirit has *ground* on which to operate, in the wicked hearts of the people. He has a right to practise his deception, and God won't stop him, but he will say, 'I am going to use that deception to bring about *my* purpose.'

Thus God does not actively add to the evil in the world, but he did set up the universe for things like that to be possible. But he is also able to use these things to get his will done in the earth. It is part of his master chess-player way of winning. Who did the killing of the firstborn in Egypt? God said *he* would do it, but it was the angel of death that actually carried it out[15]; and who is the angel of death? The devil, the one who has the 'power of death'[16]. Who prompted David to number Israel? 2 Samuel 24:1 says it was God who 'moved David', but 1 Chronicles 21:1 says it was Satan who 'moved David'. Exactly the same Hebrew word for

---

12 Psalm 82:1-2
13 Daniel 10:20-21
14 1 Kings 25:19-23
15 Exodus 11:4-5 & 23
16 Hebrews 2:14

'move' is used in both Scriptures. Is the Bible just contradictory and full of other such errors? No. Both things are said in Scripture, because *both things are true*. In exactly the way that I have just described, Satan had a right to move David, through the pride in his heart, but God was able to use it to bring about his purposes. In 2 Samuel 24, God is mentioned as the *ultimate* first cause of all things. He gives room for Satan to misuse his position and power, given to him in the first place by God, and influence David. In 1 Chronicles 21, Satan is highlighted as the *immediate* cause, the one who chooses to act rebelliously towards God and his roles for Israel, and who stirs David up to do the same. It is not that all these supernatural powers are completely out of hand and running riot. God is still on the throne, but he has to allow those around the table to fulfil the purposes for which he has created them.

Nor is it that God approves of the sickening types of destruction we see in parts of the Bible, with a kind of 'ends-justify-the-means' attitude. Jesus wept over Jerusalem; 'If only you knew the day of your visitation, but now your house is left to you desolate.'[17] When the armies of Rome came, it was the *judgment* of God but at the same time, it broke the *heart* of God. The specific violence that the Romans perpetrated as they destroyed Jerusalem, or the Babylonians smashing babies' heads against the wall as they attacked Israel[18], was *not* the ordination of God. But God, nevertheless, is ultimately responsible. As Chairman, as King, he set the whole thing up to run in this particular way. Evil incurs its own judgment, and the instrument of God's judgment sometimes causes more evil when the perverted wills of his creatures misuse their right to act in their designated realm. God is responsible, furthermore, because he keeps the whole universe running moment by moment. He supplies the energy and life that are used, even to perpetrate evil. The interaction of God the ultimate first cause,

---

17 Matthew 23:38 & Luke 19:41-44

18 Psalm 137:8-9

and the immediate causes in which our choices and wills operate, is something we have to bear in mind whenever we see these
apparent contradictions taking place in the Bible.

Think for a moment of Jesus on the cross. On one hand, the
Bible says that it was 'the judgment of God'[19] and the 'predeter-
mined counsel and wisdom of God'[20] and that 'it pleased the Lord
to bruise Him.'[21] But on the other hand, it also says that he was
'nailed to a cross by the hands of godless men'[22]. God gets his
purposes done in many ways, and sometimes he even uses evil
creatures and their evil choices to do it[23].

> *"But put forth your* hand *now and touch all that he has;
> he will surely curse you to your face." Then the Lord said
> to Satan, "Behold, all that he has is in your* hand[24], *only
> do not put forth your* hand *on him." (Job 1:11-12)*

> *"However, put forth your* hand *now, and touch his bone
> and his flesh; he will curse you to your face." So the Lord
> said to Satan, "Behold, he is in your* hand[24], *only spare
> his life." (Job 2:5-6)*

In Job 1:11 and 2:5, Satan is urging God to put his hand on Job
and bring calamity on him. But notice that in Job 1:12 and 2:6,
God says it is Satan's hand that is on Job. Many times in the book,

19 John 12:31

20 Acts 2:23

21 Isaiah 53:10

22 Acts 2:23

23 A similar metaphor is used by Tolkein in 'The Lord of the Rings'.
Evil Gollum is allowed to live to the end of the story where he finally has a dramatic part in the victory of good. In his greed for power,
he snatches the ring of power and falls with it into the Cracks of
Doom, destroying them both.

24 Many versions read 'power' for 'hand' here, but it is the same
Hebrew word as in v11

Job attributes the things that are happening to him to *God's* hand: 'Have I sinned? What have I done to you, O watcher of men? Why have you set me as your target…?'[25] We, the readers, know from the beginning that it was Satan, and not God, who was targeting Job, yet at the end of the book God commends Job by saying 'Everything you've said about me was right'.[26] Job could only understand the bigger picture of the universe, where God is overall in charge and responsible for all the things that happen in it, and in that sense he was right to attribute his suffering to God. But he couldn't see the finer detail of Satan at work through the heavenly council. That is why God challenges Job's limited perception in chapter 40: 'Will the faultfinder contend with the Almighty? Will you really annul My judgment? I made Behemoth and Leviathan, and I know how to handle them!' God was pointing out to Job in this chapter that he did not need to explain himself to Job in the running of the universe – but he also acknowledges that Job was not wrong or sinful to question the apparent conflict between the loving and protective character of God and the painful suffering he allows his creatures to experience at times. It was *Satan's* hand that was upon Job. But God brought about his purposes through it. He did not *make* Satan do the things he did, but he used it to get his will done. Of course, this is not to say that God *needs* Satan to do things so that he can get his will done; he is not dependant on him, but he *will* use the enemy's moves against him, and bring about a result that is in line with his purposes. Job's patient endurance under the affliction of Satan and his refusal to curse God in it all not only won more glory for God in proving that love is stronger than might, but is a picture of Christ himself and his attitude that won him the final victory over Satan on the cross. Don't forget that Satan is nowhere to be seen at the end of Job's story. He has been shamed and defeated by Job's response to suffering.

---

25 Job 7:20
26 Job 42:7&8

Drawing from a number of places in the Bible, the picture of the administration of the universe we see emerging is something like this: God set up the universe, and he was like the 'prime minister', or the king. He drew together a council. That council included representatives for all the things needed to run the created universe: the military, economic advisers, social welfare, and so on, or their equivalents. Each member of the council was assigned different areas of administration. Then there was a rebellion. God was still on the throne and the dissidents on the council were of his appointing, and so he could have simply dismissed them all instantly. But he chose not to. If he had, the whole infrastructure of his creation would have collapsed, and the universe he had set up would no longer exist. A new universe would emerge where only God's will was done, an autocracy where no one was really free. But love cannot reign through an autocracy. By its nature it wants to give and share. So God, in his love, allowed his original structures to continue, and he administers his rule *through* them. He allows the dissidents the areas which were already entrusted to them, and he upholds the use of their power, their forces, their rights and responsibilities, whilst all the time steering his government in such a way that ultimately his purpose of a Kingdom of love will be demonstrated. Now, that is real government!

Any other kind of government—the big fist approach, smash it all and start over again, which is what you or I would probably do—would be terrifying. If we were God, we might have thought, 'This wretched universe, what a mess it is in! Let's just throw it away. We'll get rid of that bunch there; we'll sack those rebellious angelic forces; we'll destroy the humans, there's no hope for them, they are so easily deceived. Let's start all over again.' Dictators have tried this approach throughout history. But God has *not* done that! That is why we are here! And that is why there are grey areas which we puzzle about. We sometimes wonder, like Job, why life works out like this, or why God allows particular things to happen.

A number of times in university debates I have been confronted by an atheist who has stood up and said something like, 'If God is for real, let him smite me down now!' They do not generally get smitten down, and so they sometimes feel they have won their point! But God does not do that, because God is love. And as such, he is seeking to bring about the fulfilment of the potential that he has placed in all his creatures. Premature smiting does not achieve this. God wants both the principalities and powers in the heavenly places and those who are seeking to function on earth—men, women, angels, demons, every power—to fulfil their proper potential and come to the fruition of what he made them for. And that is why we have the problems that we do. God does not give up so easily as we do.

If God had put his big fist down, we would have even bigger problems. The first time you sinned you would be written off. There would be no chance of repentance, just judgment straight away. Of course, one day God *will* bring the whole thing to a halt, and pass judgment on all his creatures. But he is waiting until the work of the cross has been extended to all so that those who receive it have something to stand on in the day of judgment. In that day, sadly, there will be those who will still insist on '*my* will be done'. But God will have to say to them, 'If you will not say, "*Your* will be done", then you had better have what you want: *your* will.' That is terrible; because *my* will, when it sets itself up against God's, only brings destruction and ultimately self-disintegration, for outside of him, there is no life [27].

Council to counsel

The heavenly 'council' is the place where 'counsel' takes place. In Hebrew the same word[28] can be used for both a 'council assem-

---

27 1 John 2:17
28 The word is *sod*

bly' and for the words, the 'counsel' that is spoken there. At the beginning of Job we are introduced to the heavenly *council*. In the next section of the book, where Job talks with his three friends and the angry young man, we meet the earthly *counsels* that are offered to Job. But as the end of the book shows us, the counsels of men are false and of no value, unless those men have been privy to the council of God, and have heard his counsel.

Jeremiah complains that the prophets had not been listening to the counsel of God. They spoke out of their own understanding, or rather their own *mis*understanding, 'saying, "peace, peace" when there was no peace'.[29] In Amos 3:7, we are told that the Lord 'does nothing, save he reveals his secret counsel[30] to his servants the prophets'. It is important for the prophets to be listening to God, because God does *nothing* unless he reveals the results of his council to them in his counsel. If the prophets have never listened to the counsel of God, they will be speaking out of their *own* understanding, and that will lead people astray. Every prophet, every preacher must spend time in the counsel of God, listening to what God is saying, how he is working to get his plans accomplished, how he intends to use the actions of his enemies to his own advantage; perhaps we could say, they are catching up on the minutes of the heavenly councils!

Psalm 82

As I have mentioned, the idea of the heavenly council is not just an obscure, one-off anomaly in the book of Job. Before finishing this chapter, we shall look more closely at two examples of it in scripture. First, let us turn to Psalm 82.

> God *takes His stand in His own congregation;*
> *He judges in the midst of the* rulers. *(v1)*

---

29 Jeremiah 6:14; 8:11; cf. 23:18 & 22

30 Hebrew word *sod* - council assembly/counsel/secret counsel

The word for 'rulers' (sometimes translated as 'powers') is the Hebrew word *'elohim'*, which is literally translated 'gods'. In fact, although the word itself is plural in form, it is exactly the same word that is used for 'God' throughout the Old Testament, including here in verse 1.[31]

> *How long will you judge unjustly,*
> *And show partiality to the wicked? (v2)*

There is a relationship indicated here between this 'heavenly congregation' and the earthly counterparts—judges, kings, and so forth—where unjust judging takes place. These spiritual powers, or 'gods', have some influence over those who should be taking account of the wicked, and dealing with them, here on earth.

> *Vindicate the weak and fatherless;*
> *Do justice to the afflicted and destitute.*
> *Rescue the weak and needy;*
> *Deliver them out of the hand of the wicked. (v3-4)*

Those who are the weak in society are being oppressed. The spiritual forces are lying behind the earthly powers of government, and are influencing them. Thus they are being instructed by God to 'vindicate, do justice, rescue and deliver' as they should be.

> *They do not know nor do they understand;*
> *They walk about in darkness;*
> *All the foundations of the earth are shaken. (v5)*

Here, we can understand these 'foundations' as the cosmic structures of the universe, the way in which God set up the earth and

---

31 Where the Hebrew reads *'elohim'* with a singular verb, we translate 'God' and where *'elohim'* with a plural verb, we can translate 'gods'.

involved supernatural powers to administrate it, giving it shape, stability and cohesion.

> *I said, 'You are gods,*
> *And all of you are sons of the Most High. (v6)*

God calls this congregation 'gods'; '*Elohim*' says to the '*elohim*', 'You are *elohim*'. There is a godlike quality about them, a heavenly relationship that exists between God and these forces he is addressing. They are even called 'sons of the Most High', and they were presumably expected to rule in the manner of their father. In this context, it is easy to understand Satan as originally being an angel, as passages like Isaiah 14 suggest. The Apostle Paul talks about him masquerading as an 'angel of light'[32], so we can imagine how slowly, around the council table, Satan ceased to demonstrate the godlike attributes of the Most High, and became more and more a rebellious 'son'.[33]

> *'Nevertheless you will die like men,*
> *And fall like any one of the princes.' (v7)*

Why will they die *like* men? Because they are *not* men. Otherwise they would die because they are men. We can see that we are meant to understand that God is addressing these 'powers', 'gods', 'sons of the Most High', angelic beings that exist around the council table of the Almighty.

---

32 2 Corinthians 11:14

33 Psalm 82:6 'sons' should not be understood to refer to the type of eternal relationship which God has with his unique son, Jesus, the Son of God. Here 'sons of the Most High' is an alternative name for 'gods' in the previous line. They are angelic creatures. The unique, eternal relationship that exists only between Jesus and the Father is marked in scripture by the phrase '*My* Son' (Hebrews 1:5)

A New Cabinet Coming!

> *Arise, O God, judge the earth!*
> *For it is You who possesses all the nations. (v8)*

The cry of the psalmist here is that God would arise and judge
these spiritual powers, thereby releasing the nations, so that the
universe could be brought back into order. And one day that will
take place! The judge of the earth will arise, and all these powers
will have to 'bow the knee and acknowledge that Jesus Christ is
Lord, to the glory of God the Father'[34].

Notice that it will not be God in his 'pure god-i-ness', who
will take back the reins - it will be God as *man* who judges, for
'all judgment is committed to the Son'[35]. Jesus earned the right
to the power and the responsibility of taking over that spiritual
government by his total obedience and Sonship demonstrated in
the cross. Therefore, he is worthy 'to take the book and sit on
the throne'[36], and this is what is meant by Hebrews 2:5; 'He did
not subject to *angels* the world to come...'. The present world is
under the subjection of angels; they function over us as the principalities and powers, the forces that we have been talking about;
they are the council of God as it appears in the beginning of the
book of Job.

However they shall give way, and the Lord will reign with a
new cabinet. The new cabinet, or council, will be those who have
been learning here on earth to reign with Christ—they have been
training for reigning. After training for reigning, these men and
women will 'inherit the Kingdom'[37], and they will 'reign with

---

34 Philippians 2:10-11
35 John 5:22
36 Revelation 5:9-13
37 Matthew 25:34

Christ'[38] for the ages to come[39]. That is the new Council.

If you and I have been seeking the kingdom first in our lives, it is we who will replace those spiritual forces in the heavenly council, because we have learned Christlike government down here on earth. The whole foundation of the universe, the structures of the principalities and powers, will be changed - no longer will it be under the subjection of angels! That is what it means for us to reign with Christ. We will judge the world, we will judge the angels together *with Christ*[40]. Do you like this idea? Well, it is God's idea! And it contributes to some of the problems we face in this life, because God continues to work through his council and not on his own.

Psalm 89

We see the heavenly council again in Psalm 89. In verses 5-8, we read,

> *And the heavens will praise Your wonders, O Lord;*
> *Your faithfulness also in the assembly of the holy ones.*
> *For who in the skies is comparable to the Lord?*
> *Who among the sons of the mighty is like the Lord,*
> *A God greatly feared in the council of the holy ones,*
> *And awesome above all those who are around Him?*
> *O Lord God of hosts*[41]...

God made the heavens, and he did not leave them empty. He filled

---

38 2 Timothy 2:12

39 Revelation 22:5

40 I Corinthians 6:2-3

41 The name 'Lord of Hosts' for God in the Old Testament is often used in the context of God's heavenly powers and his authority over them. However, the NIV translates the term 'Lord Almighty', thereby obscuring the reference to spirit beings.

them up with 'hosts' of angelic beings. Just as God made the earth and did not leave it empty; he told Adam to go and multiply, fill it up. This heavenly host is here described as 'the assembly of the holy ones', 'the sons of the mighty', and 'the council of the holy ones'. The Psalm continues in verses 8-10:

> *O Lord God of hosts, who is like You, O mighty Lord?*
> *Your faithfulness also surrounds You.*
> *You rule the swelling of the sea;*
> *When its waves rise, You still them.*
> *You Yourself crushed Rahab like one who is slain;*
> *You scattered Your enemies with Your mighty arm.*

In the Old Testament, the sea often represents the chaotic mass and movement of the spiritual forces in the universe that are hostile toward God. Rahab is a poetic and symbolic name for Egypt. The Hebrew word means 'tumult', so the Psalm describes for us a raging spiritual force, particularly dominating Egypt, and how God crushes her. He does it by the crushing work of the cross.[42] He has brought to heel that spiritual force, Rahab, the power behind the nation of Egypt, behind the powers of the Pharaohs and their magicians. We start to see how Christ's work on the cross was necessary, not only to put man right with God, but to bring the unruly principalities and powers that govern parts of the world into order.[43]

I hope you are beginning to get the idea of how God governs with this heavenly council. These thoughts have very often been abandoned in Christian thought. We often do not understand that the will of Satan, demonic wills and the wills of others play a part in the forces holding the universe together. We think and react as though it is just simply God and us. No wonder we find our theol-

---

42 Genesis 3:15
43 We see the spiritual force of Rahab in Psalm 87:4 and Isaiah 51:9.

ogy inadequate to answer some of life's biggest questions. God is working with the human race in the midst of 'hosts' of spiritual forces, some good, some evil. The human race needs releasing from those powers. That is part of the redemption Christ has brought us: he came to 'set captives free'. We are either controlled by those powers, who can then work through us, using us to judge unfairly and bring immorality and injustice into the world, or else we are standing over on the side of the Prince of Peace. We are finding his love, his goodness, his spiritual power that enables us to be the sort of people we were meant to be and to live out the sort of kingdom the world was meant to enjoy. Thus we contribute to the advance of the Kingdom of God, to the destruction of evil and to the reordering of chaos. So, are we ready to move on and get back to Job? Perhaps we will see more clearly now, in view of the sort of universe in which we live, why this poor man is going through such struggles.

Only Calvary Love is Fit to Run the Universe

Before I finish this chapter, let me just say this. The universe we live in gives rise to many forms of suffering, but Job's is of a special and particular type. As we read further, we shall discover more fully *why* it is that he is suffering. Primarily, as we discussed in chapter three, Job is demonstrating that even if you get nothing out of loving God, it is still the best way to live. It is the only way that reflects the nature of the One who gave us life in the first place. True love sits on the throne of the universe. Unless we worship altruistic Calvary Love, we will never know freedom: we will never escape the effects of 'Almighty Power' government that pushes people around and forces its will on everything that happens.

That is the battle into which the church is called. Where God sees people in the church who are blameless and upright, who are seeking to live in conformity to Christ, then sometimes he may allow them to undergo a similar battle to that of Job. You may even be in that category right now. Most of the time, we suffer because of our own wilfulness, because we push our own agenda and try to live in God's world our way instead of his. But sometimes, God calls us to suffer so that we may vindicate God's love before the heavenly realm. We declare to the principalities and powers that God is worth loving *any*way, no matter what we are going through, because his love is the only thing fit to run the world. We take our stand through suffering because we want Almighty Love to be final and pre-eminent in our life experience.

I have made the point before, and will finish with it here. With all the historic Christian creeds that exist, not one creedal statement contains those magnificent words with which the Bible uniquely describes God—'God is love.' And he is such Love that he loved the world in all its brokenness, and gave himself up for its healing and salvation. The creeds state all kinds of important truths, but none start from this foundation of the pre-eminence of God's love; yet it is the most unique facet of Christian truth. No other world religion worships a God who is, by nature, love.

Ultimately, fundamentally, when God judges, when he redeems, when he works in the universe, when he chastens us—in *everything* that he is doing—it is all out of his great, altruistic heart of Love, which he adequately demonstrated when Jesus hung on the cross. Our God points to the cross and says, 'I love you like that.' That kind of love is worth suffering for.

5

Blessing and Cursing

Then Job arose and tore his robe and shaved his head,
and he fell to the ground and worshipped. He said,
   'Naked I came from my mother's womb,
   And naked I shall return there.
The LORD gave and the LORD has taken away.
Blessed be the name of the LORD.'
Through all this Job did not sin nor did he blame God.
(1:20-22)

Job Did Not Blame God

Job's response to the disasters he encountered is remarkable. The last half of verse 22 literally reads '...nor did he ascribe unseemliness to God.' How many of us would manage to respond half as well as Job in this situation? No wonder God says, 'there is no one like him on the earth, a blameless and upright man'[1].

However, a little later on, when his friends are provoking him, he does seem to blame God and say an awful lot of things against him: 'God will not turn back his anger…if I called and he answered me, I could not believe that he was listening to my voice…he bruises me…and multiplies my wounds without cause…he will not allow me to get my breath…'[2] This produces a controversy for two reasons. First, can it be true to say that Job did not blame God nor speak ill of him? And secondly, if God can say of him at the end of the story: 'My servant Job has spoken of me what is right'[3], does this mean that it was *right* for Job to speak ill of God? And is it alright for us to do so, too?

It is important to see that God is not excusing Job's complaining. God is not here saying that we should be a continually uptight and aggressive sort of people, who are always having great arguments with God. Nor is he suggesting that it is 'right' or healthy to complain. Some current Christian pop-psychology says 'Let it all out; rage against God with your griefs and complaints and have a good go at him - he can take it!' I am sure that he can; but I do not think this is Christlike behaviour, nor do I think it is what Job is doing here.

God saw that Job was not speaking against him, he was speaking against the "god" that his friends kept telling him about; the "god" that was punishing Job because he was a sinner[4]. All the anguish of Job's heart, all the things he was grappling with, all the sorrow he felt was because he was thinking: 'How can the God I know and love be treating me like this? If my friends tell

---

1   Job 1:8
2   Job 9:13-18
3   Job 42:8
4   eg Job 4:7-9

me he is a dissatisfied and punishing God who inflicts pain on his people, then who have I been worshipping all this time?!' Job was coming to terms with a sudden realisation that the God he thought he knew, that he thought he had a relationship with, was not that God at all; it felt as if God had betrayed him, turned on him, let him down. Treachery, disloyalty, is one of the most painful things in the universe. Nothing hurts like a friend who turns out to be an enemy.

The pain that Job felt and complained of is reflective of the pain that we go through when we think we have lost God in the midst of hard times. Job thought he had lost the God that he knew. So, I don't think the book of Job gives us any encouragement to wave our fists at God every morning and complain. Rather, it teaches us to wave our clenched fists at wrong views of God - not those who hold the wrong views though! If we can make that distinction, then God will say to us, too, 'everything you spoke of me was right.'

Enter the Theologians

So, we might ask, what changed? How did Job get to this point of controversy, feeling he'd lost the God he knew, when at the beginning he wasn't complaining at all? Well, it was the *theologians* that did it! In chapter 1 he lost his family and everything he owned; in chapter 2 there was a second round in the battle, where Job himself was afflicted by Satan with 'sore boils from the sole of his foot to the crown of his head' [5] and his wife told him to 'curse God and die'[6]. He ends up sitting on the ash-heap (probably a rubbish-tip outside the city), an outcast. Then, to cap it all, his friends come along, and round three begins.

---

5   Job 2:7
6   Job 2:9

> *Now when Job's three friends heard of all this adversity that had come upon him, they came...Eliphaz the Temanite, Bildad the Shuhite, and Zophar the Naamathite...to sympathize with him and comfort him...Then they sat down on the ground with him for seven days and seven nights with no one speaking a word to him for they saw that his pain was very great. (Job 2:11-13)*

While they kept their mouths shut, these friends did a good job! But the third round comes in when Satan—having already taken Job's family and property in the first round, and attacked him physically in the second—now, through the voices of his three friends, begins to bombard Job with false theology. It is the *devil* in the mouth of Job's friends, and later Elihu, who says that *God* is causing it all. However, God *isn't*—the devil is! We know this from the introduction in chapters 1 and 2, but, of course, Job and his friends do not. Isn't that just like the devil, to try and blame somebody else? He plays on people's confusion or ignorance to make them think all bad things are God's fault, while he (the devil) gets to his evil work under cover. Jesus makes a profound comment about the source of evil and disorder in the parable of the wheat and tares[7]. The field of wheat is spoiled with tares, but not by God. Rather, Jesus says, 'An enemy has done this'. He continues by saying we cannot alter this mixture of good and evil until the end of the harvest comes. Job fights against this view of God that the devil is presenting him through the friends. It is not the God that he knows! He struggles and grapples: 'God can't be like that! If he is, he's a tyrant and unjust.'[8] And God says, effectively, at the end of the book, 'You were right Job! I would be a tyrant and unjust to have done this to you – but I didn't, and therefore, I'm *not*. Everything you have spoken of me is right.'

---

7   Matthew 13:24-30
8   eg Job 10:1-7

So, when the friends, or 'theologians' as I have been calling them,[9] start on Job with their theology, he begins to despair. Why? Because despite what they were saying, Job did not suffer because he was a sinful man. We know this again because the introduction states that Job was 'blameless, upright, fearing God, and turning away from evil'[10]. And in case we thought this was overstating it somewhat, God repeats it for us a few verses later[11]. God was not trying to humble or correct Job by afflicting him with sufferings and pain.

The Pain of Wrongly Applied Theology

Each of the attacks that Job's friends bring on him revolves around exactly this point. They all tell Job that he is suffering because he is a sinner; that God is righteous and Job ought to repent. I suppose this could sound like religious wisdom. But we must remember what sort of condition Job is in. Besides losing his family and all his possessions, Job is suffering all kinds of physical afflictions: he has itches and sores that are oozing; worms live on him; he has something like chills that make him shiver; shrivelling skin; eyes red with weeping; diarrhoea, sleeplessness, delirium, nightmares, choking, bad breath, emaciation, excruciating pain—there is a whole list, if you look carefully through the text![12] These afflictions must have been severe. But Job's great-

---

9   They are sometimes known as 'the comforters' of Job (from 2:11), though comfort seems to be the last thing they brought him! Indeed, Job himself calls them 'sorry comforters' in 16:2, and says in 21:34 that their comfort is 'vain'. Let us pray that our comforting of others is not 'vain' as theirs.

10   Job 1:1

11   Job 1:8

12   My list is not exhaustive! See J.E.Hartley Job NICOT Eerdmans Page 82

est pain seems to come when his friends cause him to question
whether he has lost God, as he knew him. The spiritual agony that
devastates his spirit begins for Job as his friends begin to speak.
The words of Eliphaz cause him to cry out 'oh' in anguish; he
starts to compare the pain erupting in his heart with the calamities
he has experienced, unable to say which is worse[13]. The *fear* of
having lost his relationship and his fellowship with God sets in;
the fear of having lost that love which at one time he thought he
knew from the Almighty. It is this that sends a tremor through his
soul, which is so dark and nihilistic he feels that he loathes his
own life[14]. The theology that was pressed upon him in an already
agonizing situation, only served to increase his anguish. It gave
Job to believe that God was absent in his suffering; God was not
with Job; he was against him; Job was a sinner and God could not
have dealings with him. These ideas caused him more pain and
distress than anything else.

People will always be caused to suffer more greatly when theology is wrongly applied to their situation. I say 'wrongly applied'
because the theology of Eliphaz, Bildad, Zophar (and later, Elihu)
is not altogether *wrong*—it is neither bad theology, nor bad philosophy—it just has absolutely and utterly nothing to do whatsoever with Job's particular situation. It may well apply to some
other people's situations, but not to Job's, as the introduction to
his book makes quite clear. Nor will this theology comfort anyone
else who finds themselves in a similar position. The problem with
the friends is that instead of being guided by the Holy Spirit to
apply their theology into Job's particular life and circumstances,
they just drop it on him, neat, as they learnt it. They seem to feel
that all they need do to speak for God is throw out the wonderful
ideas that they learned in college, or whatever the equivalent was

13 Job 6:1ff
14 Job 10:1ff

in 2000 BC. They did not look for real wisdom and guidance from the Lord as to what to say to Job specifically. They thought their bit of theological truth was good enough to meet his need. But, in fact, it was what brought the deepest suffering to Job.

Blessing and Cursing

The theme of 'cursing' flows through the first two chapters of the book of Job, and spills into the third. In Job 1:5, Job prays for his sons in case they have 'cursed God in their hearts.' In 1:11, Satan says to God that if Job is afflicted, 'he will surely curse you to your face.' This accusation is repeated in 2:5. In 2:9 Job's wife tells him to 'curse God and die!', and finally in 3:1, 'Job opened his mouth and cursed the day of his birth' (though he did not curse God). There is an awful lot to do with the mouth in those early chapters of Job, and it signals to us that it is terribly important to come to terms with the reality of our speech.

We saw earlier that we are like God in that we can make choices. That is one aspect of our Godlikeness as asserted in Genesis 1:26-27. In addition, one of the fundamental differences that separates men from animals and reveals the likeness of God in man is the ability to articulate. We have mouths that can actually speak. Genesis shows us that speech originated with God—God spoke and the universe came into being[15]. Thus it is important to underline that part of the Godlikeness of the human being is in our speech. That means that what we say is terribly important. The old adage 'sticks and stones may break my bones, but words will never hurt me' is nonsense, and everybody knows it. Words are more effective in the universe than anything else. If I speak cursing, negative speech, I bring destruction into people's hearts and minds and spirits, and this is often far more damaging and difficult to heal

15 Genesis 1:3

than anything I might have done to their bodies. Words can either
curse and destroy this world or bless it and build it up.

The words of Job's friends crushed him. Jesus said: 'My words
are spirit and they are life'.[16] Good words bring the Holy Spirit
and they bring the life of God. Bad words—cursing as opposed
to blessing—bring the enemy's power, the destructive power that
brings death into our spiritual experience. I don't know if you
have ever sensed death in a room; even, perhaps, in a church
meeting. Maybe you have smelled death in a hospital ward, or
in a home where someone has died. But sometimes when people
die who are full of the Holy Spirit, you can smell *life*. The life of
God is more powerful than the power of death. Death is a real
power; it is not simply a state, or the absence of life, it is an actual
spiritual force[17]. That is why we can experience resurrection life
in Jesus now, whereas before we were 'dead in our sins'[18]. Of
course, *physically* we were alive, but we were under the power of
death. Romans 6:23 says, 'the wages of sin is death'; a wage of
death is paid out to us every time we sin.

So, our words *release* these spiritual forces. While Job's friends
kept silent, they were good friends; but when they opened their
mouths, they became bad friends and they began to do damage.
Even a fool, according to Proverbs, is counted a wise man if
he keeps silent[19]. It is rather pragmatic in life not to rush in too
quickly with our words, thinking that we have the answer and
can put everything straight. Some people have trouble controlling
the outpouring of their words. They cannot stop themselves from
speaking. We need to discipline our mouths, so that the words we
speak release life and the Holy Spirit. We have 'the sword of the

---

16 John 6:63
17 Hebrews 2:14
18 Ephesians 2:1&5
19 Proverbs 17:28

Spirit, which is the word of God'. Our words should be like Jesus' words, spirit and life, so that when we pray into people's lives, the Spirit of God works those things we pray into them. Similarly, when we speak or preach, our words should release God's activity, by the Holy Spirit, to actually be *accomplishing* the things that we are talking about inside people.

It is possible to preach cleverly about any given topic, but that does not mean that God is actually doing it in the lives of the congregation. I am sure you have been in meetings where you have come away agreeing with everything the preacher has said, but somehow you have also felt lifeless and condemned, unable to live up to any of the things you heard. Another time, you may hear the same message, but this time you come away feeling uplifted, full of faith that you *can* live the life the Lord wants you to! There is life and encouragement released into your life. That is the activity of the Holy Spirit through the words. We want our words to be more and more *Jesus'* words—words that release the life of God into the lives and situations around us. But for that to happen, we must heed the warning presented to us by Job's friends. I'm sure they intended to say the right thing to Job, but their words were devoid of the Spirit and only weighed him down further.

Job's Birthday Curse

The tragedy is that in Job 3, when he opened his mouth, Job cursed. He did not, however, curse God; he cursed the day he was born.

> *Afterward Job opened his mouth and cursed the day of his birth. And Job said,*
> *'Let the day perish on which I was to be born,*
> *And the night which said, 'A boy is conceived.'*
> *(3:1-3)*

Sometimes our pain can drive us to a place of nihilism where we wish that we had never been born. Job is not only remembering how his body has been afflicted, and how his children, his property and his animals have all gone; he is beginning to think that his *God* has gone. This experience of God-forsakenness is surely almost impossible to endure – we can understand that it might drive someone to wish they had never been born, or even to want to end their own life. Suicidal thoughts themselves are not so wicked as giving in to them. Those kinds of thoughts are recorded here from one of the godliest men who ever lived. We need to be sympathetic with people who find themselves in that realm and try to help them, not judge them too quickly. We need to help one another not to give into the Enemy's destructive pressure in our lives; we need as many godly men and women around as possible and we do not want to lose them needlessly.

If we look closely at chapter 3, we can see that it falls into two parts: verses 1-12 are Job's curse on the day of his birth; verses 13-26 are his lament over his situation. The second section is divided from the first by the repetition of an idea that occurs at the beginning and the end of the lament, like a pair of brackets around it, enclosing it as a separate section.

> *For now I would have lain down and been quiet;*
> *I would have slept then, I would have been at rest (v13)*

> *I am not at ease, nor am I quiet,*
> *And I am not at rest, but turmoil comes. (v26)*

Both verses use the idea of quiet and rest: the first wishing for it, imagining it; the second lamenting the hard fact of its absence.

I want to look briefly now at the curse section, with the help of the insights of J.E. Hartley[20]. We can imagine that Job has been reflecting on the story of how the universe came into being that we know from Genesis 1-2, because he seems to respond to the seven days of creation as he curses his own coming into existence.

On day one of creation, God said 'Let there be light'[21]. Job retaliates with:

> *May that day be darkness;*
> *Let not God above care for it,*
> *Nor light shone on it. (Job 3:4)*

God's word separated light and darkness, night from day, but Job declares that the 'day' is 'darkness'. Job is *un*doing, or reversing, what God did in creation. In the end, any life without God will slowly destroy his created order and eventually self-destruct.

On the second day of creation, God separated the waters below from the waters above[22], and on the third day, he separated the land from the sea[23]. Previous to this, we are told that 'the earth was formless and void, and darkness was over the surface of the deep'[24].

> *Let darkness and black [deep] gloom claim it;*
> *Let a cloud settle on it. (Job 3:5)*

Job reverses this by wishing for the darkness and gloom to swallow every distinction up; for the clouds of the waters above to settle and merge with the deep below, losing the separation between the sea and sky that God created. Thus he does not need

---

20 J.E.Hartley's Commentary on Job (NICOT, Eerdmans)

21 Genesis 1:3

22 Genesis 1:6

23 Genesis 1:9

24 Genesis 1:2

to mention the reversal of day three specifically, since creation from Job's perspective is now just reverted to a deep gloom and darkness, a swirling mass of the deep where there is no earth for him to stand on anyway!

On day four, God created the sun, moon and stars, to 'govern the day and…the night'[25], and to be 'for signs, and for seasons, and for days and years'[26].

> *As for that night, let darkness seize it;*
> *Let it not rejoice among the days of the year;*
> *Let it not come into the number of the months.*
> *Behold, let that night be barren;*
> *Let no joyful shout enter it.*
> *Let those curse it who curse the day. (Job 3:6-8a)*

Now Job is dismantling the months and seasons that break up the days of the year, and both day and night are cursed. In verse 9 he adds 'Let the stars of its twilight be darkened'.

Day five of the creation story was when God filled 'the waters…with swarms of living creatures' and created 'the great sea monsters'[27].

> *Let those curse it who curse the day*
> *Who are prepared to rouse Leviathan. (Job 3:8)*

Leviathan is the great sea serpent who crops up in a number of places in the Old Testament[28]. At the end of the book of Job, Leviathan appears again[29], this time representing Satan, in serpent

---

25 Genesis 1:16

26 Genesis 1:14

27 Genesis 1:20-21

28 eg Psalm 74:13-14 and Psalm 104:26

29 Job 41:1

form as we know him from Genesis 3. Job talks of rousing the sea monster, stirring him up from the place God prepared for him at the bottom of the deep.

Day six of creation was when God said 'Let us make man in our own image'[30] and mankind came into being.

> *Why did I not die at birth,*
> *Come forth from the womb and expire? (Job 3:11)*

Job seeks to undo the creation of man, or at least his own creation, and denies the purpose, potential and destiny that God invested in mankind that they might rule on the earth.

Day seven of creation was the day of rest[31].

> *For now I would have lain down and been quiet;*
> *I would have slept then, I would have been at rest'*
> *(Job 3:13)*

Instead of moving into the 'seventh day of rest', a time to enjoy life and creation and the good things of the earth, Job looks for death and oblivion to find his peace.

Thus, bit by bit, Job has dismantled God's creation, full of order and beauty, with his words. His cursing and lamenting create a picture of life and the world that is utterly devoid of the goodness of God; he has imagined God out of the picture in his misery: 'Let God above not care for it!'[32] But God does care. Though Job's words lack hope and faith, the creation structure of Genesis 1 behind them and the beautiful poetry that he employs at least give us, the readers, cause to hope for a happier ending to the story. Perhaps all is not utterly lost; we can still find some vestige of

---

30 Genesis 1:26

31 Genesis 2:2

32 Job 3:4

beauty amidst the pain, still some evidence of the works of God in his world. In all his bitterness and discouragement, Job never cursed God, even when urged to do so because it might make him feel better[33]. Our words can be destructive and faithless, but when hedged in by a life that is seeking to be righteous and not dishonouring to God, we find that God can take even our curses and laments and birth new hope and faith from them.

In the next chapter, we shall examine in more detail the things Job's 'friends' have to say.

---

33 Job 2:9-10

6

The Earthly Counsel

How are we to comfort someone in great distress? What can we say that will bring them help or encouragement? In a moment, we shall see what we can learn from the attempts of Job's 'comforters'. But first we shall look at their counsel in the light of the overall structure of the book.

The Structure of the Book of Job

An outline of the book looks like this:

I	Ch1-2	**Prologue:** God's Council behind the scenes
II	Ch3	**Job's Curse and Lament**
III	Ch4-27	**Dialogue:** the three 'theologians'

      1. Eliphaz   - Experience

      2. Bildad   - Tradition

      3. Zophar   - Reason

Each speaks and Job replies in three cycles, except that

Zophar doesn't speak in the third cycle.

IV	Ch28	**Job's Hymn to Wisdom**
V	Ch29	**Job's Final Protest of his Innocence**
VI	Ch32-37	**Elihu, the Angry Young Man**
VII	Ch38-42	**God Answers Job:** God's theology

We have already looked at the first two chapters of Job, the prologue to the book, and also chapter 3, Job's Curse and Lament. Part III of the book takes the form of dialogue between Job and his three friends; they bombard him in turn with their theologies, first Eliphaz, then Bildad and thirdly Zophar, and in between Job answers each in turn. Then, there is a second cycle of speeches, each speaking in the same order (they are all very proper and correct!), and then a third and final cycle. In the final cycle, Zophar, who has exploded at Job rather rudely and self-righteously in the first two cycles, appears to have run out of things to say and remains silent. In fact, all their speeches generally get shorter with each cycle, perhaps as they realise that their theology has not helped Job much, and that they have nothing further to offer him.

Part IV, chapter 28, is a beautiful Hymn to Wisdom from the mouth of Job, which he follows by a great Protest of Innocence in chapters 29-31 (Part V). The protest divides into three parts: first, he *recalls his past*[1] and the honour men used to give him; secondly, he *grieves over his present*[2] state of humiliation; and thirdly, he *protests his innocence*[3] with promises and oaths. In fact, the oaths are so imposing that his friends are silenced, and the Scripture explains that 'these three men ceased answering Job, because he was righteous in his own eyes.'[4]

---

1   Job 29:1-25
2   Job 30:1-31
3   Job 31:1-40
4   Job 32:1

It is at this point that Elihu, the angry young man speaks up. Far from silenced by Job's powerful oaths of innocence, his anger burns and he proceeds to lecture Job with his own brand of theology, after the three friends have given up. His one, long speech takes up six chapters and comprises part VI of the book. It attacks Job with the same basic argument, (that Job is clearly a sinner, otherwise he wouldn't be suffering and God wouldn't be punishing him), although he does add some new - and good - ideas into the mix.

After all this, God decides that it is time *he* came in and said something, and chapters 38:1-42:6 are *God's* theology, *his* answers to Job in this the final part of the book. The speech divides into two parts, each punctuated with a short response from Job, and we shall look more closely at these wonderful answers from the mouth of God in the last part of this book.

This structure helps us to see that the vast majority of the book of Job is dialogue (or, at times, monologue). We hear Job's perspective on his suffering contrasted with Eliphaz, Bildad and Zophar's take on it, contrasted with Elihu's view, and set in the context of the narrator's wider knowledge of the action behind the scenes. Then God brings *his* perspective into the forum of their limited earthly views to comfort and encourage Job and to enable him to go on with life and walk into the time of blessing God had in store for him. Ultimately, however erudite our theology, we each individually need God's direct revelation to make sense of our lives and bring comfort to us in our suffering.

The Three Friends and Elihu

We have seen the heavenly council already in the book of Job, but now we come to the earthly counsel. What do Job's three friends and Elihu have to say to Job? Though the underlying content of their messages are basically all the same — 'Job, you're a sinner, and that's why you're suffering!' — they each approach from a unique perspective. Perhaps their perspectives are determined simply by their human dispositions. Eliphaz draws heavily from his experience of life to form his theory; Bildad likes to rely on tradition; Zophar uses reason, or common sense[5] to build up a rational argument; and Elihu makes the very important point that we need inspiration from the Almighty to shape our thinking. Experience, tradition, reason - these are all ways in which we still today might try to build our understanding of the universe, or our theology. There is nothing wrong with using any of these approaches — we use each of them when approaching the Bible, and the revelation of God[6] — but not one of them is enough on its own. Added to this, we need *God's* guidance and inspiration to put all the rest in context.

So let us look at each of the friends in turn.

Eliphaz - Experience (Experiential Theology)

Can mankind be just before God? (Job 4:17)

Eliphaz answers Job on the basis of experience. He says, in effect, 'I have had an experience, therefore I know the truth of the matter.' He is a likeable character and tries to be sympathetic to Job, though perhaps he thinks he is rather mature and is therefore a little patronising. The particular experience he has had is a dream, which he recounts in chapter 4, verses 12-21.

Now a word was brought to me stealthily,
And my ear received a whisper of it. (Job 4:12)

---

5   cf H.L. Ellison in his commentary on Job cf H.L. Ellison in his
     commentary on Job

6   John Wesley also advocated these three aspects when interpreting
     the Bible.

This is a kind of 'secret wisdom', for those in the know. You could call it a kind of 'Gnosticism'. Sometimes people talk about the 'secret of Christian living'—there is no secret at all! The good news of Jesus is open for all to know. We must beware of Gnostic ideas that distract us from the plain truths revealed to us by God.

Eliphaz continues:

> *Amid disquieting thoughts from the visions of the night,*
> *When deep sleep falls on men,*
> *Dread came upon me, and trembling,*
> *And made all my bones shake.*
> *Then a spirit passed by my face;*
> *The hair of my flesh bristled up.*
> *It stood still, but I could not discern its appearance;*
> *A form was before my eyes;*
> *There was silence, then I heard a voice. (4:13-16)*

In this beautiful piece of poetry, Eliphaz is making a big assumption: if you have a spiritual experience like that, then it must be God behind it. He thinks that, because his hair stood on end, this must be confirmation to him that it was the Spirit of God. If your hair stood on end, and your bones trembled, surely it was God you were experiencing—wasn't it? Unless, of course, it was an electric current that made your hair stand on end; or maybe you were suffering from a fever and you could not keep from shaking; or one of many other good reasons! Experience itself is not really a final conviction of the ultimate truth of the universe. Just because you have had a supernatural dream, it does not necessarily mean to say it is telling you the truth—it might be; but it also might be false. Eliphaz's message is 'you are a sinner, otherwise you would not be suffering.'[7] But he is basing that theology upon an *experience* he has had, and that alone is not adequate to get to the truth of God.

---

7 Job 4:7

I am sure you know many Christians who try to promote the Gospel simply by their experience. It is obviously a good thing to give your testimony, to say what you were and what you have become, but in the end, people claim to have experienced all sorts of things. We need to add God's words to our experience, so that our audience not only hears us but experiences the Holy Spirit backing up our words and bringing conviction and faith.

Eliphaz said he knew because he had experienced it. The trouble is, not one of us has experienced everything. How do we know that our experience is broad enough to give the full truth of the matter? Sometimes we confidently heap the knowledge of our own experience, convinced that we are right, upon people whose situation is entirely different, and for whom our experiences have no relevance. Love should always temper conviction and judgment with sympathy and understanding. It is our love that we should communicate first to those who are suffering, before we seek to inform them of why they are in that position. Unfortunately, Eliphaz, carried away in his conviction, goes on to pass judgment on Job. A voice in his dream had said:

> *Can mankind be just before God?*
> *Can a man be pure before his Maker?*
> *He puts no trust even in His servants;*
> *And against His angels He charges error. (Job 4:17-18)*

This makes it sound as though God's primary interest is to go around mistrusting and judging everybody, angels and men alike. The voice continues:

> *How much more those who dwell in houses of clay,*
> *Whose foundation is in the dust,*
> *Who are crushed before the moth!*
> *Between morning and evening they are broken in pieces;*

Unobserved, they perish forever.
Is not their tent-cord plucked up within them?
They die, yet without wisdom. (Job 4:19-21)

The inference of these words is: that is what will happen to you, Job, if you do not hurry up and repent!

Can mankind be just before God? We now know that through Jesus Christ it *is* possible to be just before your Maker. But Eliphaz concludes from the words in his dream that if anybody is suffering, like Job, it must be because he has a wrong opinion of himself, he doesn't recognise that he is a sinner and has not been sufficiently repentant. 'No man is just', therefore, if Job would only acknowledge it and repent, God might find a way of blessing him—but things will certainly not improve for him while he carries on protesting his innocence.

Of course, Eliphaz's ideas here are perfectly true—*in certain situations*. The only problem is, they have absolutely nothing whatsoever to do with *Job's* situation! Maybe Joe Brown could do with hearing them, but not Job. God has declared him 'blameless and upright' in the first chapter[8]. Eliphaz has taken his theology, some of which is true, and dropped it onto Job, as though it answered all his questions. That is *not* the way to do pastoral work! As sympathetic and as mature as he might appear to be, Eliphaz simply did not help Job by telling him he was a wicked sinner, because in his heart, Job knew it wasn't true.

Not that Job believed that he was perfectly righteous and nobody else was. He was simply asking the question, 'I think I am at least as righteous as you lot, so why is it that *I* am suffering and you are not?' We must all have had moments like this. Has someone ever come up to you when you have had some trauma in

8 Job 1:8

your life, put their arm around your shoulder and said something
like, 'Now, brother, now sister, this is all in love, but you really
ought to repent'? Or perhaps the old favourite, 'God is chastening
you, friend.' I don't know about you, maybe I am just particularly
unholy, but I immediately think, 'Well, why doesn't he chasten
you, then? Where are the tragedies in your life? Why me?' Now,
I know people are often well-meaning when they say these things
– like Eliphaz, they are looking for something helpful to say into
your situation. But it is very arrogant to say, in effect 'You need
God's chastening a whole lot more than I do!' In all his arguments
and defences, Job is really saying 'I know I am certainly not more
wicked than you people, I may even be a little bit better; so why
me?' If we are honest, that question goes through most of our
minds when we are suffering. Why me and not them? And if suffering was always just a question of chastening, then it is a very
reasonable question. If God is chastening me to make me a bit
more holy, then he could equally well be chastening these others
around me. They need to be made more holy just as much as I do.
But, as we know, suffering is not only a question of chastening,
we may experience it for many different reasons.

Another Reason for Suffering

Eliphaz's main contribution to the argument is, 'No human is
righteous before God – therefore we suffer because we are not
penitent enough.' If we suffer a terrible experience in our life, it is
not a bad thing to ask the Lord, 'Have I done something wrong?'
But the answer is not always, 'Yes, you have, my child, and I am
chastening you.' Sometimes, as we have already touched upon,
the answer is far more profound. We are demonstrating love
before eyes of the universe, just as Jesus did when he was on the
cross, and just as we, his body, are still also at times called to do.
We shall continue to unpack this idea as we go along.

Remember that Jesus did not suffer all through his life—the experience of the cross lasted about six hours. There were times in his life when he was 'rejoicing with great joy'[9]. We should not expect to spend our whole lives suffering, but there may be times when we are called upon to endure hardship—not because we are sinners, not because we are being chastened, not because we are not right with God, but because God is proving to Satan that despite all his attempts to make it otherwise, there are people who will love like Calvary, like God loves. That message must be declared loud and clear before all the angelic powers and heavenly forces, so that they know that real love does exist—not only in God, but that it is being reproduced in *man*, who is made in his image. Job's friends didn't leave room for this as they formulated their theologies; they couldn't see beyond 'If you suffer, you must be a sinner.' Thus the experiential stance that Eliphaz took toward the situation is not adequate.

Bildad – Tradition (Traditional Theology)

Does God pervert justice? (Job 8:3)

Our next friend, or theologian is Bildad. Unlike Eliphaz, Bildad does not come with any sympathy at all. Straight away he launches into Job, quite insensitively:

How long will you say these things,
And the words of your mouth be a mighty wind?
(Job 8:2)

A few sentences later the word 'please'[10] is used, but he isn't *asking* Job nicely—he means, 'You should jolly well do it!' Bildad is really the archetypical, non-compassionate 'Pharisee'.

9   eg Luke 10:21
10 Job 8:8

You can just picture him, after his initial indignant outburst, trying to appear benevolent and compassionate by saying '*Please, Job…*' He carries on:

> *Does God pervert justice*
> *Or does the Almighty pervert what is right?*
> *If your sons sinned against Him,*
> *Then He delivered them into the power of their transgression.*
> *If you would seek God*
> *And implore the compassion of the Almighty,*
> *If you are pure and upright,* (Implying 'As I am!')
> *Surely now He would rouse Himself for you*
> *And restore your righteous estate.*
> *Though your beginning was insignificant,*
> *Yet your end will increase greatly. (Job 8:3-7)*

Satan's attack on Job through Bildad and his misapplied theology is to say that God never perverts justice[11] which is obviously true, but again, does not apply to Job's particular circumstances. Moreover, Bildad is still saying exactly the same thing as Eliphaz: 'Job, you are suffering because you are a sinner', just in a slightly different way. This time, the reason given is because of God's justice. Eliphaz had said that no human being was righteous before God, therefore the suffering was for chastening; Bildad now says that God never perverts justice, therefore Job must deserve his suffering for being a particularly wicked sinner[12].

Tradition

To justify his arguments, Bildad appeals to tradition. In verses 8-10 he says,

---

11 Job 8:3
12 Job 8:20

Please inquire of past generations,
And consider the things searched out by their fathers.
For we are only of yesterday and know nothing,
Because our days on earth are as a shadow.
Will they not teach you and tell you,
And bring forth words from their minds? (Job 8:8-10)

People often try to build their understanding of the universe, their theology, and thus their value system on the strength of tradition. Bildad's appeal is 'Everybody knows what I am saying because it is traditional, God has always been understood this way; there must be a good reason for these views to be handed down thus, so why go against years of accepted beliefs?'

At first it may sound very humble and commendable to say that our lives are brief and that we know very little compared to the accumulated wisdom of the sages of the past. But it is not so wise to use their conclusions drawn from their time, from their particular situation, and apply them without any thought to current circumstances. Tradition is a ground of authority for many religious people to which they adhere with pride; and that pride can escalate until it is impossible for them to allow deviation even an inch from what has been taught and handed down over the years.

Of course, it is important to take heed of what has been taught in the past, but if it becomes the only measure of truth and stops us from moving on with what God is doing throughout the sweep of history, then we are opening ourselves up to deception. If we had adhered solely to Christian tradition, the Reformation would have never taken place; John Wycliffe would never have translated the whole Bible into English and we would only have the Latin version; and we would never have rediscovered the power of the Holy Spirit in the Restoration days of the last couple of hundred years. To depend entirely upon tradition to guide us into all truth will stop us from moving forward with what God is trying to do in the church today.

Jesus warned us against the hypocrisy of clinging to tradition instead of listening to God. The Pharisees were so proud of their religious history, worshipping the past and building impressive tombs and monuments to the great men and prophets of old[13]. But Jesus said that setting up tombs for prophets is exactly what the Pharisees of old did too – after putting to death those whose message they didn't want to hear. And no more would the Pharisees in Jesus' day have listened to the prophets' message, had they been alive at the time; they would have stuck with the traditions of *that* time, and killed them all. The prophets were a new, and often unpopular voice in their own day, because their message would carry a warning from God to repent from the ways people were used to living and return to God's way.

People who are a little pharisaic often appeal to the past for wisdom. Bildad says 'Look to past generations…we are only of yesterday…our days on earth are as a shadow…'[14] But surely the saints of the past lived just as briefly as we do and were generally just as ignorant, just fallible as us. They were unlikely to have come up with answers that are any more profound and eternal than ours might be, simply because they existed before us. It sounds humble to say 'we know nothing in comparison'[15] but it is not really true.

Having said that, it is important for us to build for the future on the foundations of the past. We shouldn't throw everything out and start again with each new generation. There is an awful lot

---

13 Matthew 23:29-31
14 Job 8:8-9
15 Job 8:9

we can learn from those who have loved the Lord before us, and we ignore it to our peril. C. S. Lewis once said that we should read at least two old books for every modern one, in order to keep a proper perspective on our current time. If we count the people of the past as fools or irrelevant, and only to listen to the current ideas of the day, we risk missing the direction of the progressive movement of what God is doing through history to get his purposes worked out on the earth. If you are given a map with a marked destination, you need to know roughly where you started out on it in order to locate your current position and then move nearer to your goal. Our Christian history with its successes and its failures will help us to understand where we are at now so that we can press on to where God wants us to be – a church that looks like the bride that he longs to return for!

To sum up, Bildad says, 'Tradition has always said that sinners suffer because God is punishing them: God cannot pervert justice, so Job must be suffering justly in God's eyes.' It is perfectly right to say that 'God may deliver us into the power of our transgression'[16] - but we have been told that Job was not suffering on account of his sin[17]. Just like Eliphaz, Bildad, has misapplied the things he has learnt about God. His answers are 'one size fits all'. Let us seek to avoid applying answers in a blanket fashion to every new situation that faces us, however much tradition has upheld them, without taking time to hear God regarding the current, individual circumstances.

Zophar - Reason (Rational Theology)

Can you discover the depths of God? (Job 11:7)

If Bildad was unsympathetic and insensitive, Zophar comes across

16 Job 8:4
17 Job 1:8

as arrogant, pugnacious and rude! I am sure you do not know any
Christians like that! His first response to poor, suffering Job is:

> *Shall a multitude of words go unanswered,*
> *And a talkative man be acquitted?*
> *Shall your boasts silence men?*
> *And shall you scoff and none rebuke? (Job 11:2-3)*

He charges Job with being 'talkative', yet in his self-righteous
anger Zophar himself pours forth 'a multitude of words'!

> *For you have said, `My teaching is pure,*
> *And I am innocent in your eyes.'*
> *But would that God might speak,*
> *And open His lips against you,*
> *And show you the secrets of wisdom! (Job 11:4-6a)*

In other words, 'if *God* would speak - oh, then you'd be in trouble, Job! He'd soon cut you down to size!'

> *For sound wisdom has two sides.*
> *Know then that God forgets a part of your iniquity.*
> *Can you discover the depths of God?*
> *Can you discover the limits of the Almighty?*
> *They are high as the heavens, what can you do?*
> *Deeper than Sheol, what can you know? (Job 11:6b-8)*

Or perhaps, 'How could you possibly understand anything, you
miserable pea-brain?!' Zophar is angry with Job: he has heard
him reject the arguments of Eliphaz and Bildad comes in burning
with indignation. Each time a new cycle of arguments unfolds,
the friends' speeches get shorter as they start to run out of words;
but Zophar's are always the shortest, two fiery outbursts of blus-
tering infuriation until he burns himself out and remains totally
silent for the third cycle.

Zophar seems to be exasperated at Job's lack of what we might call good, down-to-earth common-sense; the sort of thing that people are generally agreed upon as being true in life. He bases his argument on sensible rationality. 'It stands to reason' would be a popular phrase with him. He makes everything out to be so self-evident:

> *Can you discover the depths of God?*
> *Can you discover the limits of the Almighty? (Job 11:7)*

'You don't know everything, Job! Surely any reasonable man knows that there are *limitations* to what we can understand of the infinite God? If things in life appear contradictory to you, so what?—God is *beyond* reason. If you think your suffering is unreasonable, use your reason to see that God is *above* reason and rationality. There are some things we simply have no answers for.'

This is a strange attitude, but we can find it in many popular exponents of Christianity. They argue a case, for example 'God is love', until something contradicts it, for example 'so why does he allow us to suffer?', and the response is, 'well, God is a great, inscrutable mystery, all apparent contradictions make sense in him, we just can't understand it.' Why should we reason at all if in the end God is beyond reason? God is not beyond reason: 'In the beginning was the Word'[18], Greek *logos*, where we get our word 'logic' from.

Zophar nevertheless continues.

> *They are high as the heavens, what can you do?*
> *Deeper than Sheol, what can you know?*
> *Its measure is longer than the earth,*

---

18 John1:1

And broader than the sea.
If He passes by or shuts up,
Or calls an assembly, who can restrain Him?
For He knows false men,
And He sees iniquity without investigating.
(Job 11:8-11)

Zophar is saying there are things that God knows that Job knows nothing about. This is true as far as it goes. But the implication is: Zophar also knows – at least more than Job does. When we say to somebody that God is so vast we cannot possibly understand him, it may sound very humble, but if we are using it as a means of getting our theological point across, we are really saying, 'God is too big for *your* reason, but *I* have got enough reason to see that I'm right and you are wrong!' Zophar is saying, in one breath, that God and his ways are past knowing; and yet in the next, that he knows enough of those ways to say that Job is a sinner, and that is why he is suffering! Perhaps you may have met that kind of arrogance, and found it rather disturbing. Nevertheless, that is the way that Zophar tries to make his point.

The climax of his argument is:

And an idiot will become intelligent
When the foal of a wild donkey is born a man.
(Job 11:12)

'Job, you are a donkey! No, less than that, you are the off-spring of a donkey; a donkey's donkey! Not just an ass, a baby ass!' Zophar has got himself terribly worked up and now he is simply resorting to abusive language. Job is reduced to this silly ass who does not have enough intelligence to sit down and think things through until he agrees with what Zophar already knows – there are no answers to Job's questions about his suffering, because

God is too big for that. That is the essence of the false argument that Zophar is trying to put over.

Zophar appeals to reason and rationality for his argument. Yet again, underneath it all is the same assumption that Eliphaz and Bildad held: 'God makes the wicked suffer.[19]' He then adds his own particular twist: 'You may question this, Job. You may wonder how you can deserve *this much* suffering, or why others seem to be judged better than you, but ultimately there are no answers to that. It's plain to see that God, in his wisdom, is simply too big for us to understand!'

Never Stop Thinking

It is fascinating to see the individual personalities of these three 'friends' or 'comforters' coming through in their approach to thinking through the big questions of life. Sympathetic Eliphaz speaks primarily from his own experience. Pharisaic Bildad holds fast to tradition. Plain-speaking Zophar prefers the common sense approach. And these three approaches are all useful to us in unravelling the complexities of life. We can learn from our experience, we should value our traditions, we ought not to neglect our common sense.

Ultimately, we are never meant to stop thinking. We are never meant to stop searching for Spirit-filled wisdom and reaching out harder and further after God. One of the things lacking in the lives of many ordinary Christians today—apart from a deeper and greater love for one another!—is good thinking. We do not reason out our faith enough, so that when we are asked for an opinion on an important subject, we do not know what to say. Or when we are challenged with lies that undermine our faith, we are too

19 Job 20:29

uncertain and afraid to give a rebuttal. Worse still, we are so used to disagreeing and clashing with one another that we never expect to come to a great conviction of the truth on any given matter; we never speak out boldly, 'This is the word of the Lord!' Because we have not studied the truth, we do not have the confidence to express what the Bible says on any particular issue. We hope that our Sunday School grasp of the truth of Jesus will be good enough for the rest of our lives. But if you are an architect, an engineer, a biochemist or a barrister, you would expect to spend your whole life using your God-given brain cells to try to grasp and better understand what it is that you are doing, so that you can grow in expertise in your field and go on doing it better. Why should it be any different for disciples, learners, in the life-long school of Christ? We should be continually asking questions, getting into his truth, studying the Scriptures, so that we *know what we believe*, and we can say why we believe it with conviction.

'Do not be children in your thinking; yet in evil be babes, but in your thinking be mature', says Paul in 1 Corinthians 14:20. 'In understanding be men' is how the old Authorised Version put it. Job's three friends have helpfully shown us that we can take initial steps to come to truth with our experience, our traditions, and our reason. But they also set us up for the final contribution from the 'earthly counsel' who will introduce us to something vitally important that all the others missed.

Elihu – Holy Spirit (Inspirational / Revelational Theology)

'The Spirit[20] of the Almighty gives understanding'
(Job 32:8)

Elihu is the final man to offer Job counsel in his suffering. Some

---

20 Often translated 'breath' – 'breath' and 'spirit' are the same Hebrew word *ruach*

commentators maintain that all four men speak the same message: that Job is suffering because he is a sinner. That is true on a basic level, but as we have seen, they each arrive at that conclusion from their own particular perspective. Elihu, too, has his own approach, and it is very productive because he touches on the real root of the problem. The other friends never acknowledge that they need *inspiration* to know how to apply their theology. They just formulated their theories, based on truth, and imposed them upon Job carte blanche. But Elihu maintains that the reason they have not persuaded Job with their answers to his 'preposterous claim to innocence'[21] is that they are trying to argue against him *without the help of the Holy Spirit*[22]. Now, that is an advance in our reasoning.

I have already made the point that we must not drop our theology, our ready-made answers upon people without first asking the Lord to help us and to show us what, how and when we should say it. Otherwise, all too often what we say will not apply or appear relevant. We need the Spirit of God to illuminate and guide us as we impart what we know. We need the Holy Spirit to give us answers—not only when we are being questioned, challenged or persecuted[23]—but also when we are trying to do pastoral work. We need the inspiration of the Holy Spirit to be able to apply truth to a hurting person in a way that will meet their need and bring them release. This may at times be confrontational—the Lord does lead us like that in some situations. But it will always be in such a way as to bring life, healing and wholeness to the person, not more pain, depression and bondage. It is not enough to say, 'Well, I have given them all I have got; they know the truth now and it's not my fault if they don't listen to me!' We must seek to

---

21 Job 35:2

22 Job 33:4

23 Matthew 10:17-20

use the tool of God's word with the skill of the Holy Spirit to get into the *heart* and *life* of such people, and reach them in such a way that their problem is answered. Paul calls the Holy Spirit 'the Spirit of Wisdom and revelation in the knowledge of Christ'[24] because he understood that we need the Spirit to 'lead us into'[25] all truth.

Obviously, we shall still find recalcitrant and adamantine hearts that will not give way to the truth of the Gospel and our desire to see them blessed—sadly, there are people like that. But at the same time, there are a lot of people who are not blessed, helped and taken on with the Lord because they are treated in the wrong way. It is always helpful to ask, as pastors or as those trying to do pastoral work, 'Lord, could I have put that another way? Could I have found the particular truth that really meets this need? How can I communicate it so that it will resonate with this particular person?' *We cannot do this by ourselves.* We need God with us, guiding us as we apply truth so that people are *delivered* from their problems.

The 'Angry Young Man'

The three cycles of speeches between Job and his three friends finish at chapter 27, and Job's final 'summing up' for them starts sarcastically: 'What a help you are to the weak!...What helpful insight you have abundantly provided!'[26] He then embarks upon his beautiful poem, or 'Hymn to Wisdom' in chapter 28, before finally protesting his innocence with great oaths in chapters 29-31. Job's speech where he swears to his purity and his innocence before God is dramatic and awe-inspiring. So much so that it

---

24 Ephesians 1:17
25 John 16:13
26 Job 26:1&3

finally leaves the three verbose friends speechless. Their arguments have not worked and they have run out of things to say.

> *Then these three men ceased answering Job, because he was righteous in his own eyes. (Job 32:1)*

Elihu, however, was far from deterred.

> *But the anger of Elihu the son of Barachel the Buzite, of the family of Ram burned; against Job his anger burned, because he justified himself before God. And his anger burned against his three friends because they had found no answer, and yet had condemned Job. Now Elihu had waited to speak to Job because they were years older than he. And when Elihu saw that there was no answer in the mouth of the three men his anger burned. (Job 32:2-5)*

His anger burned. We ought to give thought to our own attitudes. It is love, not anger or frustration, that is necessary to reach into people's real needs. We are told that Elihu was younger than Job and the three friends, and that he was angry because the friends had no answer for Job. Younger men can often get angry with their elders for not having, or at least not appearing to have, all the answers. The arrogance of youth often believes it knows everything; it can see through all the mistakes of its elders, and usually put them down to the changing times with which they cannot keep up. But when they reach old age, they will find that they do not have all the answers either. As Solomon said, 'There is nothing new under the sun'[27]. The mistakes of past generations will be similarly repeated by the next, however well-informed and on-the-button they think they are.

---

27 Ecclesiastes1:9

Presumably, Elihu thinks he is 'burning on God's behalf'[28]. Angry young men and women are packed full with emotion; but emotion is not the same thing as the Holy Spirit. Although Elihu interprets it as the Holy Spirit, in actual fact, his anger and emotion get in the way and confuse the issue in the end. However, I am not writing this angry young man off entirely. He does help us to get closer to the truth. Revelation from heaven by the Holy Spirit was necessary for the answers to Job's questions. But Elihu's anger, far from supporting his point, leads him off track and causes him to once again miss the point: Job isn't suffering because of his sinfulness, there is something more profound going on.

I don't want to be too negative about angry young men. I was one myself once, many years ago! God directs his rebukes in the final chapters of the book at the three older friends of Job, but he says nothing about the angry young man. I find that encouraging. God can deal with angry and arrogant young people who burn 'for the Lord's sake'. They can turn out to be sweet natured characters by the time they die, and if they maintain the zeal for him that they started out with, when he has finished refining them, they can be great workers for him. Thank the Lord for that!

It is angry *old* men that we have to be worried about! I like George Muller's prayer, 'Lord save me from becoming a wicked old man'—I am praying that these days! God seems more ready to tell the older ones off for their unhelpful theologising. Perhaps because they should have known better at their age! But it seems he could put up with Elihu; he had time ahead of him to change. I like to think he turned out to be very useful to the Lord in the end.

So, in spite of the fact that Elihu confused the Holy Spirit with his own emotion, he did bring this important truth:

---

28 Job 36:2

But it is a spirit in man,
And the breath of the Almighty gives them understanding.
(Job 32:8)

The Spirit of God has made me,
And the breath of the Almighty gives me life. (Job 33:4)

When the spirit (or breath[29]) of man touches the Spirit of God, there is *inspiration*. When God's Spirit and our spirit meet by God *breathing* into us, then 'the breath of the Almighty gives' us 'understanding'[30] and that is revelation. Whether or not Elihu actually uses this knowledge, nevertheless, his words are true. We need the inspiration of the Holy Spirit when it comes to understanding and applying truth.

This is important when we come to handle the Word of God. We do not read the Bible as simply a cerebral book from which we can draw out doctrines. It has been said that an atheist could readily understand all the doctrines of the Christian faith if he took the trouble to read and study the Bible. This is not true: we need the 'Spirit of wisdom and of revelation in the full knowledge of Christ'[31] if we are to know 'the truth as it is in Jesus'. We need inspiration to *understand* as well as inspiration to *apply*. We need the 'Spirit of God' and the 'spirit in man' to be brought together and 'the breath of the Almighty to give us understanding'[32].

Before we leave Elihu for the moment, (he has something further to contribute, which we shall look at later), let us note what he says in verse 10 of chapter 32:

So I say, 'Listen to me,
I too will tell what I think.'

---

29 'Spirit' and 'breath' are the same Hebrew word, *ruach*
30 Job 32:8
31 Ephesians 1:17
32 You might like to meditate on Luke 9:51-56

Hopefully, if we make bold statements like these, what we think will be what the Spirit has been inspiring us with. But in the end it turns out in Elihu's case that all he had to share was his own personal thoughts on Job's situation: 'Job, you are suffering because you are sinful!'[33] This is exactly what all the others said, and though he delivers it with a great deal of verbiage and passion, we are shown that it simply is not true of Job's case.

Four Ways We Interpret Scripture

Let us pause here for a moment and notice what we can learn from these four men about how to read and interpret Scripture. John Wesley taught the first three principles, and the fourth he assumed.

1. Experience

Some Christians like to make a big fuss about 'Scripture speaking for itself' – in other words, if we come to read the Bible without our own presuppositions, we will all come up with the same, unquestionable truths. This is not true. Not one of us can come to the Scripture without reading it through a lens of our own experience of life and of the things that God has done with us. This is not bad, nor is it wrong, it is inevitable, and can be helpful, especially for discovering the impact of the words of Scripture in our day-to-day lives. But we have to acknowledge that our different lenses will sometimes lead us to different interpretations of the truth. If one man has never seen God do a miracle of healing, nor met anyone else who has, he will be tempted to read the stories of lame men walking and blind eyes opening in the book of Acts and conclude that the Holy Spirit is not doing that kind of work today; it was a special experience, just for the first century Apos-

33 Job 33:8-22

tles. On the other hand, if another man has laid hands on the sick in Jesus' name and seen them recover before his very eyes, he will disagree with the first man's interpretation of Acts; the Holy Spirit does indeed still work through us with miracles of healing today! Neither experience necessarily proves the case – we need the Holy Spirit to speak to our hearts, to reveal to us what God is doing in his world today and how it relates to the stories we read in his Word. We cannot rely on experience alone to interpret the Scripture correctly.

2. Tradition

When we come to the Scripture, we stand in a stream of centuries of godly people who have meditated upon it and taught it to others. It is important that we take this into account, because, whether directly or indirectly, these people influence us. No matter how 'non-traditional' some might think they are, they can never fully escape what they have picked up from someone else's teaching, example or writings, who in turn has picked things up from someone else and so on. People influence one another, and we all stand in some tradition or other, whether or not we know it.

The Christian Creeds we have developed over the centuries seek to sum up the major doctrines that the thinking worshippers of the early church held to. Those doctrines were gathered from as near the time of Jesus and the birth of the early church as possible, and so we can trust that they are pretty reliable representations of the gospel in its purest form, before too many heresies had time to develop and pollute the message. However, as I said earlier, not one of those Creeds ever stated the primacy of love in the nature of God. 'That in all things He might have the pre-eminence'[34]. 'He' refers back to what we translate as the 'beloved Son' of a

---

34 Colossians 1:18

few verses earlier[35]. The Greek literally calls him the 'Son of His love'. It is he who is at the heart of the message of Christianity. Love is who God is.

We should not continually try to re-invent the wheel as we study the Bible and try to understand it. Men and women of the past have done great work in drawing out truths that will help us as we seek to apply it to our lives. However, there may yet be more of the depths and the love of our wonderful God to be discovered. As the *Mayflower* sailed off to the States, John Robinson said, 'There is yet more light to break forth from God's Word.' Tradition is important, but it is not final. There may be truth that the Spirit of God will lead out of the Scripture, and take us on in.

3. Mind / Reason

It may seem obvious, but when approaching the Bible we have to use our minds. The traditions of Islam do not teach Muslims to read the Koran in this way. They have to memorise and recite it in its original form, whether or not they read or understand Arabic. Many Muslims can recite huge portions of the Koran without understanding a word of what they are saying. Similarly, there are some Christians, who are genuine, godly and spiritual people, who say that to believe the Word of God must override reason. So, for example, if the Bible says that the world was created in seven 'days', it must be true and they must be literal days, whether or not science, archaeology and rational investigation prove something different. But reason does not have to conflict with what we read in Scripture, and most reasonable scholars have no problem interpreting the first few chapters of Genesis so that it is both compatible with scientific discovery whilst at the same time revealing important truths for us about mankind's creation,

---

35 Colossians 1:13

purpose and destiny. The truth is, we cannot even *read* the Bible without using our reason. Our minds help us to take it in and understand it – we must not think we have to dispense with them altogether. The mind is an *instrument* that God has given us; we are meant to use it to worship him[36].

Of course, reason alone will not lead us into all the truth of Scripture. Proverbs 26:4 tells us '*Do not* answer a fool according to his folly!', but the very next verse says '*Do* answer a fool according to his folly!' Reason would tell us it is impossible to follow both these instructions at the same time. We need the Holy Spirit to tell us when each truth applies. Jesus' disciples sometimes found their reasoning got in the way of hearing the truth of what Jesus was telling them. As Jesus prophesied his betrayal and death, Peter could not see how this would achieve the purpose of the Son of God who came to bring salvation to the world[37]. It made no sense to him and he rebuked Jesus. We cannot base all our theology on reason; we must *use* our reason to get to grips with the text of Scripture.

4. Holy Spirit Inspiration

When we interpret the Bible, we use our experience, tradition, and our reason; but above all we must invite the help of the *Holy Spirit*. It is the Holy Spirit who leads us into all truth[38]. Whenever I turn to the Scripture for my daily devotions and whenever I study it, I do so in prayer, in conversation with the Lord. I always say to Bible School students: 'Write your essays on your knees!' We need God to illuminate the text with the light of His Spirit, otherwise we shall be in danger of turning out like Eliphaz, Bildad or

---

36 Mark 12:30

37 Mark 8:27-33

38 John16:13

Zophar—'Biblical Pharisees'. We think we know it all, we have read all the right commentaries and we can put everybody in their place and beat them in argument. It's a good feeling, isn't it, to win a theological argument; to see them twist and squirm as you use the truth of God to put them down and show them you were right and they were wrong? You go back home with a great feeling of satisfaction, until God speaks to you and tells you how he was heart-broken to see you behave in such a manner toward your brother or your sister.

That is not what the Word of God was given to us for. It was given to us for obedience, for truth, for revelation to others. It was given to us to bless and share with one another; not to put people straight and prove ourselves right. Unfortunately, some people's whole idea of Christianity is that they need to prove they are right and everybody else is wrong. But truth is meant to do good, not to destroy people. Of course, sometimes it will perform a little surgery in our lives and remove a few 'cancers'. But it was never meant for decapitation.

So, all four of Job's contenders show us a different means of finding truth. Isn't it both amazing and encouraging that each one of these men of God had something to contribute to our understanding? We can learn something from each of them, in spite of their failures, if we will just read beyond their fleshly dispositions, their limited revelation and their less than perfect behaviour with the eyes of the Holy Spirit. And we can pray that God will use us too, in spite of our failings and imperfections, to teach something of his truth to others.

Allusions to Jesus

To finish this chapter, let us return to Elihu for two further contributions he makes in his argument.

1. Job needs a Mediator

> *If there is an angel as mediator for him,*
> *One out of a thousand,*
> *To remind a man what is right for him,*
> *Then let him be gracious to him, and say, 'Deliver him*
> *from going down to the pit,*
> *I have found a ransom';*
> *Let his flesh become fresher than in youth,*
> *Let him return to the days of his youthful vigor;*
> *Then he will pray to God, and He will accept him,*
> *That he may see His face with joy,*
> *And He may restore His righteousness to man.*
> *He will sing to men and say, 'I have sinned and perverted*
> *what is right,*
> *And it is not proper for me.*
> *He has redeemed my soul from going to the pit,*
> *And my life shall see the light.' (Job 33:23-28)*

Elihu says there is a mediator, a unique angel, one in a thousand. The word 'angel' in both Hebrew and Greek simply means 'messenger'. John the Baptist was called an 'angel'[39]. They couldn't have been referring to his shiny clothes and heavenly appearance – he lived in the desert wearing a leather jacket and eating locusts! He was a messenger. Jesus, too, is prophesied to be an 'angel/messenger of the Covenant'[40]. The New Testament picks this idea up as a 'mediator', one who stands between God and man and seeks to bring them together into a covenant relationship[41]. Elihu saw that mankind needed a mediator who could talk things through for God and man and find a ransom for us, so that we could have a right to come before God. This picture is, of course, ultimately fulfilled in Jesus. Even though Elihu could not see how

---

39 Greek *angelos* cf Matthew 11:10, Mark 1:2 & Luke 7:27

40 Malachi 3:1

41 Hebrews 8:6; 9:15; 12:24; 1 Timothy 2:5; Galatians 3:19

his words would be fulfilled, he depicted the need for a mediator very clearly, with prophetic insight. And now we, on the other side of the incarnation, can look back on his words and know that the one he wished for has come in Christ.

2. Job needs God to judge him with lovingkindness

> *Whether for correction, or for His world,*
> *Or for lovingkindness, He causes it to happen.*
> *(Job 37:13)*

Elihu says that God judges[42], but that he does it with *lovingkindness*[43]. Once again, Elihu manages to go one step further than the three friends in shedding further revelation upon Job's suffering. His diagnosis of Job's situation is still wrong - he thinks Job is a wicked sinner, and so he cannot really answer Job in his questioning – but he does get one vital thing right. He says that what God does, he does out of lovingkindness. It is not simply out of anger and hatred for sin that God punishes people and sends suffering upon them. It is out of his lovingkindness, his love for Job, that God is judging him like this. Elihu may not have got it all right; he still thinks that Job is suffering because he is a sinner. But at least he is aware of God's love, his covenant faithfulness, and that this motivates everything he does. This must have been a reassuring piece of revelation to Job who was beginning to feel he had lost the loving God that he knew because of the suffering he was enduring. And of course, we know that this picture of a merciful judge is finally fulfilled in Jesus – the righteous judge[44] - who primarily came into the world not to judge it, but to save it because of the love which the Father who sent him felt for his people[45].

Elihu's glimpses of the need for a mediator and a judge who

---

42 Job 36:31
43 Job 37:13
44 2 Timothy 4:8
45 John 3:16-17

offers lovingkindness are just two of many other allusions to Jesus throughout the story of Job's suffering. The following chapters will develop this theme. We shall see that Jesus is absolutely necessary to bring an answer to Job's suffering. We shall also see how the pictures of Jesus in Job's story point us to an answer as to why he was suffering at all. Job himself has a glimpse of the answer, even before God has spoken, when he speaks out those famous words:

> *I know that my Redeemer lives,*
> *And at the last He will take His stand upon the earth.*
> *Even after my skin is destroyed*
> *Yet from my flesh I shall see God;*
> *Whom I myself shall behold... (Job 19:25-27a)*

By faith, by the Holy Spirit at work in his heart, Job knows he has a Redeemer, a mediator who has the power to bring him into the presence of the Almighty God, even after his death. Even in the midst of his sufferings, truth begins to be born in his heart and life concerning why he is where he is and what his future holds.

7

The Revelation of Jesus in Suffering

The Rock Beneath our Feet

Where is God when it hurts? Where is he when I am drowning and lost in the pain of my circumstances? Does he care? How could he possibly know what it feels like? How can *he* relate to *me*? What could he possibly have to say that could comfort me?

Before God finally turns up in the whirlwind, at the end of the book, and gives his answer to Job's questions, Job is struggling. We saw how he came to the place in his pain where he wished he had never been born. He cursed the day of his birth. He lamented over what he had lost. And then, to make matters worse, his friends, who should have been helping him and bringing him comfort, instead made him feel that he had lost the God he thought he knew. Thus Job goes deeper and deeper into the pain of his own being. But it is *in that pain* that he begins to find some glimmers of hope, some hints at answers.

They are not as clear or comprehensive as the final answer that God would bring. But they are like pin-pricks of light breaking through into the darkness of Job's existence. Many who have suffered can testify to this experience. The pain causes us to think that God is miles away until we cry out, 'My God, my God, *why* have you forsaken me?!' But as we speak those very words, we find we are making contact with a God who has stepped into our place of pain in Christ. A little flash, a spark of illumination appears in our difficulty, as the Spirit of God draws close to us. It takes us by surprise. Of these times, Faith, my wife, wrote:

Days of Pain

I thought I could not face the days of pain alone again
It seemed too much for any mortal, crumbling frame to bear
But He knew better
And in my lonely valley of despair
When even life itself became a fetter
I found Him there
He did not come to me in robes of light
Or joy too bitter sweet
But in my sorrow's night
When down a dark and slippery path I trod
I found a rock beneath my feet
And knew that it was God.

Job is walking a similar path himself through these chapters. But every now and again, as we read his plaintive speeches of sorrow and despair, we find a flash of hope and we see that Job knows his feet are touching something solid. He does not always know what it is, but we shall find that that rock, which comes out in his reaction to the things his friends are telling him—that rock beneath his feet is, of course, the One who declares, 'If you build on my words, then you build upon a rock.'[1] When the storm comes, we will find, as Job did, that there is a rock under our feet: He who is *the* Rock.[2] This man, probably not even a Jew, but living around the time of Abraham, crying out to God 2,000 years before Jesus was to be born, finds under his feet the rock, whom we know as Christ the Lord[3].

We are going to look at seven places where these glimmers of light break through to Job in his sufferings. For it is through them that he starts to see how God might meet his need, and even identify with him—*understand* him—in his sufferings. The first six points pick up on different stages of our Lord's life and ministry: his incarnation, life and teaching ministry, death, resurrection, ascension and second coming[4]. The seventh point takes a look at the Hymn to Wisdom which comprises chapter 28 of Job.

1. Incarnation – Umpire

For He is not a man as I am that I may answer Him,
That we may go to court together.
There is no umpire between us,
Who may lay his hand upon us both. (Job 9:32-33)

Where do we turn when we suffer? What solutions do we seek to try to alleviate things, if at all possible? In chapter 9, Job mentions

---

1   Luke 6:47-48

2   Psalm 18:2; 1 Corinthians 10:4

3   If Job was only written down in the days of Hezekiah (8 BC), or even later, its 'Sitz im Leben' is Patriarchal (1800-2000 BC).

4   I encountered this approach in Campbell Morgan's *Answers of Jesus to Job*, and have somewhat expanded it.

some of the physical suffering with which he has been afflicted:

> *He will not allow me to get my breath,*
> *But saturates me with bitterness. (Job 9:18)*

Asthma has grasped him, he is panting for breath, he despises his life[5], so he starts to blame God, or rather the *image* of God that has been presented to him by the theologians:

> *It is all one; therefore I say,*
> *'He destroys the guiltless and the wicked.'*
> *If the scourge kills suddenly,*
> *He mocks the despair of the innocent.*
> *The earth is given into the hand of the wicked;*
> *He covers the faces of its judges. (Job 9:22-24a)*

> *Wickedness is ruling the roost, there is no justice to be found. If it is not He, then who is it? (Job 9:24b)*

There, Job asks the key question! 'If God is not doing this to me, then who *is?*' *We* know that it is Satan[6], Job, however, does *not* know. So he comes up with his own possible solutions to his suffering.

> *Though I say, 'I will forget my complaint,*
> *I will leave off my sad countenance and be cheerful,'*
> *I am afraid of all my pains,*
> *I know that You will not acquit me.*
> *I am accounted wicked,*
> *Why then should I toil in vain? (Job 9:27-29)*

The power of positive thinking – where we often turn when the chips are down. Here you are, wanting to die, and inevitably some-

---

5   Job 9:21
6   Job 2:6

one will always suggest, 'Come on, put a brave face on it! Pretend you are happy even if you are not! Say a few cheerful, positive words to yourself and you will feel a lot better!' It's a common enough suggestion, but it does not really work when you are in *real* trouble, as Job seems to have found out when he tried it.

So he tried something else:

> *If I should wash myself with snow*
> *And cleanse my hands with lye,*
> *Yet You would plunge me into the pit,*
> *And my own clothes would abhor me. (Job 9:30-31)*

This time he turns to some kind of religious remedy. A spot of ritual washing—as some might view baptism today – recite the Lord's Prayer, or visit a confessional. The hope is that engaging in religious behaviour will produce an inner cleansing that will ease the suffering. But neither positive thinking nor religious rituals have the power to change Job or his situation.

So, Job finally turns to the one for whom he keeps looking, throughout the book, and he gets his first flash of light:

> *For He is not a man as I am that I may answer Him,*
> *That we may go to court together.*
> *There is no umpire between us,*
> *Who may lay his hand upon us both. (Job 9:32-33)*

2,000 years before Jesus came, in the midst of complaining and bemoaning his situation, Job, a suffering man, suddenly realises with a flash of revelation, 'What I need is somebody who can put one hand on me and one hand on God; someone who can fully represent both of us, and thus bring us together.' There is no other adequate way for God and man to meet. There is no better way for Creator and creature to relate to each other. If we are to find a solution to the problem of evil and suffering, the things that divide man from God, making him feel guilty and unworthy, or cheated and alone, we need somebody who can stand equally with man *and* with God; someone to act as a fair and just umpire; someone who can adequately represent both deity *and* humanity. Job is longing for an incarnate God, a God who has taken to Himself the body of a man.

Umpire

There is no other solution in this universe for anyone who has been touched by evil and pain. Job was overwhelmed with pain. He was being told it must be because he was evil. He was wracking his brain for a way to take up his case before God, but he knew he really had no right to approach him. Then suddenly he thought, 'I need an umpire, *someone who is not biased one way more than the other.*' It is Jesus he longs for; the incarnate God, revealing himself, his character, his personality, his purposes, in the only language we can understand, the language of humanity. Job was unsure that such a one existed, but he had at least begun to find hope for a solution to his suffering.

2. Identification – Deliverer

> *Have You eyes of flesh?*
> *Or do You see as a man sees?*
> *Are Your days as the days of a mortal,*
> *Or Your years as man's years,*
> *That You should seek for my guilt,*
> *And search after my sin?*
> *According to Your knowledge I am indeed not guilty;*
> *Yet there is no deliverance from Your hand. (Job 10:4-7)*

What does God know of the realities of human life and human

suffering? How can he, being almighty, relate to what I have to go through each day? How could he possibly understand the fear of pain or death? And therefore, how can he have the right to judge us at all?

Perhaps, if we are honest, these questions are familiar to some of us when we are in great pain or trouble. Job asked them too, though, instead of asking them *about* God, he asked them *to* God. And in this very act of appealing to God in the midst of his pain, another flash of inspiration came through.

> *Have You eyes of flesh?*
> *Or do You see as a man sees? (Job 10:4)*

Although Job thinks the answer is *No*, deep inside he senses the answer *ought* to be *Yes*.

> *Are Your days as the days of a mortal,*
> *Or Your years as man's years? (v. 5)*

How can the immortal understand what it is to be a mortal? How can he who sees all things know what it is to have the limited view-point of a creature? In short, how can God *really* know what it is to be a human being? We have moved on here from the idea of incarnation alone. Job is asking: can God *really* know what it is to be *mortal*? To know what it is to have your days numbered, and to live out a life on earth? Can he *really* identify completely with us?

There is a lovely hymn that starts:

> *And didst Thou love the race that loved not Thee?*
> *And didst Thou take to Heaven a human brow?*

It continues in the next verse:

> *O God, O Kinsman, loved, but not enough!*
> *O Man, with eyes majestic after death,*
> *Whose feet have toiled along our pathways rough,*
> *Whose lips drawn human breath*[7].

The moving poetry describes the wonder not just of the incarnational, but the mortal life of Jesus—who knows what it is to be a man, living out a life; eating, bleeding, living like we live. If, like some of the Hindu gods, God had merely appeared in the form of a man for a short time and then disappeared again, we could not count that as truly experiencing what it is to be human—not compared to our God who had to walk the pathways of this life from childhood, had to tread on *our* roads with *our* feet, dirty and calloused; a God who knows what it is to feel strength and skill growing in his hands as he learns carpentry in his foster-father's shop. It is no comparison to the one who sat on the hills of Galilee and began to teach, knowing that he had only a short space of perhaps three years in which to get it all across, before he would be killed. The kind of God who merely 'appears' as a man is not able to give an adequate answer to the sorts of situations which you and I face, or which Job faced in these chapters. Job asked "Is there a God who has counted his years, who knows how long a day can feel, who has lived in the same scene as I have, who is not just an apparition or an appearance, but a real, flesh and blood man?" And he concluded that the answer *may* be *No*, but that it *should* be *Yes:* there has got to be a God like this! If not, there is little point in finding a God at all.

There is a picture I love that hangs in my study, which two friends of mine gave me for my birthday. It is by Millais, who

---

7   From *Poems*, by Jean Ingelow, 1863.

spent years studying the muscles of a carpenter in order to paint Joseph in the carpenter's shop. Next to Joseph it depicts Jesus as a boy, obviously helping him work; he has cut the palm of his hand with the carpentry tools. There is our God! He is so truly human that he had to grow up and live all those years as a child, and learn things. He would have been told by his foster-father: 'Now, don't use the chisel that way, you have got to always chisel away from you ... that's right; now, be careful ... now look, you have cut your hand!' In the picture, his cousin John is also there with a bowl of water, as the blood drips onto Jesus' foot. His mother Mary is consoling him, and Mary's mother is depicted too. Ominous shadows lurk in the room which holds more than enough wood for a cross.

I wonder how many times Joseph had to say to Jesus 'You always plane with the grain!' (although, I don't suppose it sounded as quaint as that!)? Jesus had to be taught how to handle wood and masonry. You learn by your mistakes— but these are not sins. As a child, Jesus must have learned how to walk, and fallen over many times, even bruised his knees... and this is the God that we worship! So, later on in his ministry Jesus explains to the people: 'I do nothing but what I see My Father doing; and I always say what My Father is saying.'[8] He had learned that in the carpenter's shop, and was still saying it as he ministered the presence of his Father into the lives of the people around him; 'If you have seen me, you have seen the Father.'[9] Obedience is very important, even God himself has learned it.[10] Isn't that wonderful?

As he walked and taught, we see the very *ministry*, the *service* of our Lord in his humanity as he identified with humans and their

---

8   cf John 5:19 & 7:16-18

9   cf John 14:9

10 cf Hebrews 5:8, 'Although He was a Son, He learned obedience from the things which He suffered.'

humble state. James probably first heard much of the teaching he later wrote down in his epistle as he was with Jesus in the carpenter's shop. Perhaps they were talking as they knocked a nail into a bit of wood, or cut out a mortise joint. James learnt from his elder brother, who was a real man, really teaching, as much a human as ever we are. 'That is the sort of God I want,' says Job in chapters 9 and 10—a God who is God and man; and a God of ministry, of serving. Not just a God who has *become* a human being, but a God who has identified with the whole of human being and its earthly predicament in order that he might salvage it.

This is the Jesus whom one day we shall meet face to face in the resurrection. We shall *know* that he has lived the whole human life, even into death, and then out again into resurrection. God *still has that body!* He took it up into heaven with him at the ascension. The eternal God looks out into the universe in the person of his Son, and sees things as we see them, with the 'eyes of a man'. This is the supreme uniqueness of our wonderful Christian faith!

There are theists and deists in the church who are reluctant to make too much of Jesus. It can be controversial to talk about him, and more people can relate and accept what we say if we always talk in terms of 'God'. Jesus is controversial; but he is the God that we proclaim! 'If you have seen me, you have seen the Father.'[11] Let us never stop talking Jesus-talk. It is a figment of the imagination to think it is *superior* to talk of 'the Almighty Creator of heaven and earth'. We would not have a clue who he was had he not come and revealed himself to us. And when he did, he came as the man, Jesus. I made the point earlier: we know nothing about God unless he tells us what he is like.[12]

We do know a lot about Jesus. When people say, 'I don't think

11 John 14:9
12 Job 11:7

Jesus is God'—how do they know? We don't know what God is like unless he reveals himself—so how can they say Jesus isn't him? Jesus claims to be that very revelation of God. I reckon he is head and shoulders above any human being that I have ever seen, so perhaps there is more to him! That is how the Galilean fishermen found that he was God. That is what brought Thomas to make his great confession at the end of John's gospel, "My Lord and my God!"[13] We should call him 'Confessing Thomas', rather than 'Doubting Thomas' after a statement like that! He could make it because he had followed him, from the first, with the fishermen and the tax-collectors; and day by day, Jesus was growing in his sight, until eventually the truth of what he was looking at filled him: 'My Lord, and My God.'

It is Jesus who can show us who God is. Without him we know next to nothing about God. We might know something about his power; we may know some wonderful facts about the creation he made - quantum physics, or that the angles at the base of an isosceles triangle are always equal—but we know *nothing* about the *character* of God, nor about his person, save we come to Jesus. It is there that we see the Father—*that* is what he is like.

Our Deliverer

Jesus had brothers and sisters; he lived with his mother and his foster-father, and presumably supported his mother after Joseph died. He experienced all the hardships of life and family. This is a God who can truly relate to us. In Job chapter 9, as Jesus' incarnation was alluded to, his role as an *umpire* was being emphasised. Here, as Jesus' life and ministry are in view, it is a *deliverer* Job seeks:

> *According to Your knowledge I am indeed not guilty;*
> *Yet there is no deliverance from Your hand. (Job 10:7)*

---

13 John 20:28

By identifying with fallen humanity God has delivered mankind. The life, ministry and teaching of Jesus show us the way to deliverance. 'Everyone who comes to me, and hears my words, and acts on them, builds on a rock—and when the storms come, they shall not collapse.'[14] We have a God who has lived through all the storms of a human life and thus who is able to deliver us from the midst of them.

3. Crucifixion – Saviour

> *Though He slay me, I will hope in Him.*
> *Nevertheless I will argue my ways before Him.*
> *This also will be my salvation,*
> *For a godless man may not come before His presence.*
> *(Job 13:15-16)*

This is Job almost at the end of his tether. He feels that he is almost dead, and is beginning to think: 'What if God goes all the way, and *kills* me?' He is confronted by the reality of the borders of his finite existence. Yet in that very moment, he flickers up with hope and faith, declaring: 'Even if God kills me, I am going to hang on to him! I think he still is worth trusting, even if I die—but I will still want to know why!'

This has to be the final zenith of hope; hope brought to its total climax where it becomes faith, the assurance of things hoped for[15]. It is the same faith we see in Jesus, who 'perfected faith'[16] when he hung on the cross and cried out, 'Why?!'[17] Before he went to the cross, Jesus knew he had come to die and what it was to accomplish, and he taught these truths to his disciples who found

---

14 See Matthew 7:24-27, and Luke 6:47-49.
15 Hebrews 11:1
16 Hebrews 12:2
17 Mark 15:34

it hard to understand[18]. But as he hung on the cross, 'treated as sin for us'[19], and the sins of the world were laid upon Him, he cried out 'Why?'. His mind was totally darkened; all that it rationally knew before was obliterated as he experienced the agony of carrying the sins of the world and went into hell and judgment and into the final repudiation of man condemned by God. Bearing the sin of the world brought an inevitable *confusion*, because that is the nature of sin. Sin takes away our understanding and darkens the mind[20]. In the place of sin, Jesus cried out 'My God, My God, *why?*' He knew why. We can read about it in the first part of the story. But hanging on the cross, he no longer knew *why*, because the darkness of sin and its consequences, its near oblivion, was such that he could hardly understand what was happening. There it was that Jesus said in his heart, like Job, 'Though He slay me, *yet* will I hope in Him.' That is where Jesus has been; and *that* is the perfection of faith.

Jesus is 'the author and perfecter', the completer, the champion of our faith[21]. If you think your faith is about to fail because your plight is so hopeless, go back to Jesus; he has much of it! He has won faith, and can minister it perfectly, by the Spirit of faith, into your heart and life. Paul talks of the 'Spirit of faith' in 2 Corinthians 4:13-14 saying that it can raise us up, just as it raised Christ from the dead. Wesley sings:

> *Spirit of faith, come down, Reveal the things of God;*
> *And make to us the Godhead known,*
> *And witness with the blood:*

I couldn't put it much better. As we call out 'Spirit of faith, come!', faith rises up in us: 'Though he slay me, yet will I hope

18 Matthew 20:17-28
19 2 Corinthians 5:21
20 2 Corinthians 4:4
21 Hebrews 12:2

in him.' There was a rock under Job's feet at those very moments when he thought he had lost his footing for good. All was not lost; something was still holding him. It was a God who now has been in that very place where all seems lost, yet who has come out the other side of death and into life again in resurrection power. He can minister to us, in our confusion and darkness, because though slain, he lived to stand in God's presence to argue his case and ours by identification. That is the place of salvation that Job was looking for beyond the grave and that Jesus secured for us. For his case was unassailable as his life was perfect.

Saviour

Appropriately, in this context of salvation and an allusion to Christ's crucifixion[22], we find one of 14 places in the Old Testament where all three Hebrew words for sin are mentioned together, painting us a picture of sin in its totality:

> *How many are my* iniquities[23] *and* sins[24]*?*
> *Make known to me my* rebellion[25] *and my* sin[24]*.*
> *(Job 13:23)*

In Leviticus in the passage on the great 'day of Atonement', those three words are again used together for a comprehensive analysis of what sin is:

> *Then Aaron shall lay both of his hands on the head of the live goat, and confess over it all the* iniquities[23] *of the sons of Israel, and all their* transgressions[25] *in regard to all their* sins[24]; *and he shall lay them on the head of the goat and send it away... (Lev. 16:21)*

---

22 Job 13:15-16

23 Hebrew *avon*

24 Hebrew *chattath*

25 Hebrew *pesha* can be translated 'rebellion' or 'transgression'

'Iniquities' are 'perversions', where we have taken what is good and twisted it; 'transgressions' are our 'rebellious acts', where we wilfully deviate from the path God intended for us; 'sins' are more generally where we miss the mark, we stray, perhaps unintentionally, from that path, or we fall short of the standards God expects. The trio appears again in the famous 'Suffering Servant' passages in Isaiah, prophesying the coming of the Messiah:

> *Surely our griefs He Himself bore,*
> *And our sorrows He carried;*
> *Yet we ourselves esteemed Him stricken,*
> *Smitten of God, and afflicted.*
> *But He was pierced through for our* transgressions[26],
> *He was crushed for our* iniquities[27];
> *The chastening for our well-being fell upon Him,*
> *And by His scourging we are healed.*
> *All of us like sheep have* gone astray,[28]
> *Each of us has turned to his own way;*
> *But the Lord has caused the* iniquity[27] *of us all*
> *To fall on Him…*
> *…As a result of the anguish of His soul,*
> *He will see it and be satisfied;*
> *By His knowledge, the Righteous One,*
> *My Servant, will justify the many,*
> *As He will bear their* iniquities[27].
> *Therefore, I will allot Him a portion with the great,*
> *And He will divide the booty with the strong;*
> *Because He poured out Himself to death,*
> *And was numbered with the* transgressors[26];

---

26 Hebrew *pesha*

27 Hebrew *avon*

28 This phrase evokes the idea of *chattath* 'straying sin'

> *Yet He Himself bore the sin[29] of many,*
> *And interceded for the transgressors.*
> *(Isaiah 53:4-6 & 11-12)*

In Jesus, our Messiah, the wonderful Suffering Servant, *all* our sins are carried away. He was cut off for *all* our transgressions, he bore *all* our iniquities. However you define sin, whichever way you have fallen foul of it, he has fully dealt with it all. That is the God that Isaiah prophesied and Jesus fulfilled; the same kind of God that Job needed and was crying out for thousands of years before.

4. Resurrection – Lover

> *Oh that You would hide me in Sheol,*
> *That You would conceal me until Your wrath returns to You,*
> *That You would set a limit for me and remember me!*
> *If a man dies, will he live again?*
> *All the days of my struggle I will wait,*
> *Until my change comes.*
> *You will call, and I will answer You;*
> *You will long for the work of Your hands. (Job 14:13-15)*

Before we look at these great words regarding resurrection, let us look at their context. In Job 14:7, Job continues his complaint:

> *For there is hope for a tree,*
> *When it is cut down, that it will sprout again,*
> *And its shoots will not fail.*
> *Though its roots grow old in the ground,*
> *And its stump dies in the dry soil,*
> *At the scent of water it will flourish*
> *And put forth sprigs like a plant. (Job 14:7-9)*

---

29 Hebrew *chattath*

So, trees are alright—there is always some hope for them! Though they are cut down, maybe at the scent of water they will sprout again. The big question is:

But man dies and lies prostrate.
Man expires, and where is he?
As water evaporates from the sea,
And a river becomes parched and dried up,
So man lies down and does not rise.
Until the heavens are no longer,
He will not awake nor be aroused out of his sleep.
(Job 14:10-12)

Man seems less advantaged than the tree. We are not able to 'rise again', we seem destined to lie down in the sleep of death, never to be roused.

But look closer! At the very point of saying this, something is happening in Job's life. First he says in verse 13, 'Oh that You would hide me in Sheol' (the place of the departed, where those who die go)—he is asking God to hide him in that place where there would be no more pain and suffering for him. 'That You would conceal me'—in other words, tuck him away, put him 'to bed', that he might sleep and be troubled no longer—'until Your wrath returns to You'—until God feels better about him. 'That You would set a limit for me and remember me'—Job wants God to put a 'marker' in Sheol, to remind him of Job when his wrath has cooled.

And then he says:

If a man dies, will he live again?
All the days of my struggle I will wait,
Until my change comes.
You will call, and I will answer You;
You will long for the work of Your hands. (Job 14:14-15)

'Until my *change* comes'—the Hebrew root is the same as we saw in verse 7, when it says of the tree that 'it *will sprout again*'[30]. Job says he will wait until he 'sprouts again'.

'If a man dies, will he live again?' Of course, Job, along with the rest of the ancient world, thinks that the answer is *No*. But he *wishes* it could be *Yes*. It is not that Job exactly believes in a resurrection in these verses; it is more that he thinks there *ought to be* one. It is his desire, the longing of his heart, and as he cries out to God, talking it over with him, there comes to him a spark of revelation. 'You will call and I will answer you' – from the grave! – 'You will long for the work of your hands' – the human bodies sown perishable God will raise imperishable![31] Whether or not he realises it himself, he prophesies the great day of the final resurrection that Jesus explains to us will one day come[32]. Job felt if there could only be a future hope of resurrection, he could endure all the days of the 'struggle' of his existence on earth.

Lover

Job's great dream-solution for his problems is that God could tuck him up in Sheol, away from all the pain and pressure, until his anger had passed. Then eventually the time would come when God would long for Job again, like a lover, and *'call'* him, and *'change'* him. Jesus nearly quotes Job when he says, '...all who are in the tombs shall hear His voice, and shall come forth to a resurrection of life, or of judgment'[32]. Paul reminds us that when the trumpet sounds 'the dead in Christ shall rise' and 'we shall all be changed'.[33]

---

30 Hebrew root *chalaph*
31 1 Corinthians 15:42
32 John 5:28-29
33 1 Thess. 4:16; 1 Cor. 15:51-52.

There are only two clear references in the Old Testament to a general resurrection:

> *Many of those who sleep in the dust of the ground will awake, these to everlasting life, but the others to disgrace and everlasting contempt. Those who have insight will shine brightly like the brightness of the expanse of heaven, and those who lead the many to righteousness, like the stars forever and ever. (Daniel 12:2-3)*

> *Your dead will live; Their corpses will rise. You who lie in the dust, awake and shout for joy, For your dew is as the dew of the dawn, And the earth will give birth to the departed spirits. (Isaiah 26:19)*

Apart from these, we see the resurrection in the Old Testament only in 'types', that is, stories or people that the New Testament picks up and interprets in the light of resurrection, largely with reference to the Messiah.

For example, Isaac was said to be 'given back in resurrection' from the Mount of Moriah.[34] Jonah, swallowed by the fish and, after three days, spat out again is called a sign of Christ's resurrection.[35] Why was resurrection not clearly understood in Old Testament times[36], but is now clear to us in the New Testament? Because Christ has 'brought life and immortality to light through the gospel'[37]. In other words, by his own resurrection, he has now given us an understanding of the days to come, of resurrection and of life and immortality. For if the head of the body (Christ) has

---

34 Genesis 22 and Hebrews 11:17-19.

35 Jonah 1:17 (and see his prayer in Jonah 2) and Matthew 12:39-40.

36 Other Old Testament verses relevant to resurrection are Genesis 3:15; Psalm 16:9-11; Hosea 6:1-2

37 2 Timothy 1:10

been resurrected, then the rest of the body will inevitably follow (the Church, the Body of Christ). That is the sure hope we have! Job said he needed a God of resurrection; and that is the God we have in Christ Jesus.

5. Ascension – Advocate

> *Even now, behold, my witness is in heaven,*
> *And my advocate is on high...*
> *...O that a man might plead with God*
> *As a man with his neighbour! (Job 16:19 & 21)*

Have you ever felt that life is unfair? Have you ever known that you were in the right, but somehow nobody could see it your way or believe you? You feel exasperated, and if you try to justify yourself you can see your hearers thinking, 'But there is always another side...there's no smoke without fire!' and no one stands with you. That is exactly how Job felt. In chapter 16, he cries out,

> *O earth, do not cover my blood,*
> *And let there be no resting place for my cry.*
> *(Job 16:18)*

He wanted there to be a permanent testimony, a reminder to all left on the earth, of the pain, the agony and the suffering he had gone through.

> *Even now, behold, my witness is in heaven,*
> *And my advocate is on high.*
> *My friends are my scoffers;*
> *My eye weeps to God.*
> *O that a man might plead with God*
> *As a man with his neighbour! (Job19-21)*

Job complains: 'There is nobody who will speak for me, my friends are all against me. Who will join with me and appeal to God: "God, when will you do something about this?!"'

No one will stand with Job and say he is not a sinner. They don't want to support Job in his suffering in case he really is in the wrong and then God might turn on them next. They are all like sycophantic 'yes-men', who want to get over onto the side of the Almighty and butter him up to be nice to them. Their 'allegiance' to God is because they think he is bigger and stronger than the devil. We all want to be on the side of whoever is the biggest and strongest. But that is not the kind of allegiance God wants. He wants us to stand on his side because we love him and he loves us, because he is good and true and right, regardless of whether he is the strongest. He *is* the strongest, but that is not the reason he wants us to stand with him. He wants us to do it out of love; not *fear* or *self interest*. Because he is *good,* not fearsome. Because he is *love,* not just almighty and able to bless us.

Job believed that there must be *someone somewhere* who knew that he was in the right and would be willing to stand with him; a witness to the truth. There must be *somebody* who understood his situation and knew that he was pure-hearted; that he was not the deceitful, crafty, wicked person that his 'friends' made him out to be. So he said, 'I have a witness, but I'm not finding him here on earth, so that witness must be in heaven!'

Who in the New Testament is called the 'witness' of God? Jesus is the 'faithful witness' in Revelation 1:5; the 'faithful and true witness' in Revelation 3:14. He is called the witness of God because everything about him witnesses to who God is. Jesus also said, '...the Scriptures...bear witness of me'[38]. So, the Bible points to Jesus, and Jesus points to the Father. Jesus is the witness who is *now* in heaven.

---

38 John 5:39

The Lord in heaven knows all the secrets of our hearts. If ever you are innocent, yet people paint an opposite picture of you, putting you in the wrong; if ever you feel frustrated that nobody is standing with you, and you are misunderstood, cry out with Job, 'My witness is in heaven!' Jesus knows how you stand before him and he is faithful so that one day, everything hidden will be brought to light.[39]

Advocate

Job calls this witness his 'advocate on high'.[40] An advocate is some-body who pleads for us, in a law-court situation. When I am being held up and accused or blamed before a judge, I need an advocate to defend me, someone who is *for* me. Hebrews 7:25 tells us that Jesus 'ever lives to make intercession for us'. Romans 8:34 agrees that 'Christ Jesus is He who died, yes, rather who was raised, who is at the right hand of God, who also intercedes for us'.

At this very moment there is a man in the heart of God who is pleading, interceding, for mankind. He is there because after his resurrection from the dead, he ascended on high and sat down at the right hand of the Father. 'We have an Advocate with the Father, Jesus Christ the righteous'.[41] That same man is called a *witness* because he has seen our plight and knows it first hand. In the law-courts of heaven, we have someone who speaks for us as human beings; an advocate and witness who is a man. What is more, that man, Jesus, is also 'in the Father'[42], so that his witness is in the heart of God itself. God's own heart witnesses for us; he is no longer against us. God is *for* us, *genuinely* for us. And 'if God is for us, who can be against us?'[43]

---

39 Matthew 10:26

40 Job 16:19

41 I John 2:1

42 John 10:38

43 Romans 8:31 (NIV)

Perhaps this illustration will help: as God's heart beats, it is as though it is pumping out 'eternal life...eternal life...eternal life...' But now there is also a man in the heart of God. Jesus went back to be with his Father, but he never put down his human body[44]; he took it with him into heaven, and therefore into God! Thus there ever lives in the heart of God the person of a man. That is why now when God's heart pumps, 'eternal life...eternal life...eternal life...', it does so *through a man,* through a human being. It truly beats: 'for humankind...for humankind...for humankind...' The heartbeat of God is now *towards* us, because Jesus lives and intercedes for us, our ascended Advocate with the Father. It is that heartbeat that pumps out God's Spirit into the earth as at Pentecost.

That is the work of Christ at the moment. He cried, 'It is finished!' on the cross, as he completed the work of reconciliation, but that does not mean he has stopped working! He is not relaxing in heaven! He is pleading for mankind! He is there, in the heart of God, forming God's heart into the shape of a human being.

In Job 16:21, Job says, 'O that a man might plead with God as a man with his neighbour!' We can know our God as close as a neighbour! He is near to us, he has lived amongst us, he has been one of us. Our neighbour, now, is in God's heart pleading humanity's case. Job needed a God like that, but did not know where to find him. We do.

6. Second Coming – Kinsman-Redeemer

And as for me, I know that my Redeemer lives,
And at the last He will take His stand on the earth.
Even after my skin is destroyed,
Yet from my flesh I shall see God;

---

44 Luke 24:50-53

Whom I myself shall behold,
And whom my eyes shall see and not another.
(Job 19:25-27b)

Job wants his words to last forever:

> *Oh that my words were written! Oh that they were inscribed in a book! That with an iron stylus and lead They were engraved in the rock forever! (Job 19:23-24)*

Not only does he want the words chipped out in stone, like the Ten Commandments, but also filled up with lead, to make sure it *stays* that way for people can read it. He is upset that no one around him is reading his story right; nobody can answer his problem. So he wants to leave it for generations to come, to read it (as we are!) and see if they can find the answer.

As we have listened to Job's words in his suffering, the revelations, or sparks, or glimpses he gets of the One who is to come, our Lord Jesus, have taken us through his incarnation, his ministry, his crucifixion, his resurrection, and his ascension. Now, finally, we have reached the Second Coming.

Kinsman-Redeemer

> *And as for me, I know that my Redeemer lives,*
> *And at the last He will take His stand on the earth.*
> *(Job 19: 25)*

There will be a day when our God comes again in Jesus, and puts his feet once more upon the earth. That day will be the day of judgment. Zechariah prophesies: 'And in that day His feet will stand on the Mount of Olives...the LORD, my God, will come, and all the holy ones with Him!'[45]

---

45 Zechariah 14:4-9

'Even after my skin is destroyed, yet from my flesh I shall see God.'[46] Job is talking about a point after death, when nevertheless he shall see God from out of a body. Although 'flesh and blood cannot inherit the kingdom of God'[47] we will have a body in eternity, an 'imperishable body'[48], and this will come about after Jesus comes again.[49]

I love Job 19:27. Probably the best literal translation is:

> *"Whom I shall see to be on my side,*
> *And whom my eyes will see to be un-estranged."[50]*

In other words, God will not be a stranger! The 'God' that Job's friends keep talking about, who beats him up for being a sinner when really he is innocent, is a stranger to Job. That is why he complains that he feels far off from God. But he holds onto the hope that one day he will see God, face to face, when he comes again, and the God he sees will not be a stranger. He will be the God that Job thought he knew, before his friends started working on him. He will be the God who is just and good, the one with whom he had a real relationship.

There is a lovely hymn that speaks about finally arriving at the glory of heaven, and it says,

---

46 Job 19:26

47 1 Corinthians 15:50

48 1 Corinthians 15:42

49 1 Corinthians 15:22-24

50 For example ASV, 'Whom I, even I, shall see, on my side, And mine eyes shall behold, and not as a stranger'; or, beautifully translated in the NJB, 'He whom I shall see will take my part: my eyes will be gazing on no stranger.'

There no stranger-God will greet thee;
Stranger thou to courts above
He who to His rest shall greet thee
Greets thee with a well-known love[51].

Job had lost the God he thought he knew. This song, however, sings about meeting God in the future. His love will be a well-known love because we have known him, and worked with him, and walked with him on earth. Similarly, Job's hope is that, at the last, his God will come again, and Job will see that he is really not a stranger to him, but is for him and on his side. Centuries before Jesus came, Job was longing for the God of the Second Coming!

7. Eternal Wisdom

This chapter began with the assertion that there were at least six places in the book of Job where his sufferings led him to realise that the sort of God he needed was the one who we know will appear in the New Testament two thousand years later - Jesus. Now we shall turn to this seventh place of inspiration in Job, the Hymn to Wisdom in chapter 28.

Although Job's protesting continues after the last speech of the three friends, Bildad's in chapter 25, and continues through to chapter 31 after which Elihu takes up the onslaught, virtually all commentators remove chapter 28 from Job and speak of it as a separate poem dedicated to wisdom by an unnamed author. This is probably correct. The language employed is so different in style and content from that of any of the speeches so far. However, its placement in the midst of Job's last major complaint does not have to be viewed as an insertion that should not be put into Job's mouth at all. It could be that Job is using this hymn to strengthen

---

51 From the hymn beginning "Rise my soul, thy God directs thee" by J.N. Darby

himself as he searches for wisdom in his predicament. Singing this hymn to wisdom in the middle of his trouble is thus understandable, especially to those of us who daily use hymns to sustain our walk with God. Jesus too used Psalms to express his heart and derive comfort on the cross, Psalm 22:1 "My God, my God, why have you forsaken me?" and Psalm 31:5 "Into your hands I commit my spirit". Perhaps he was also reciting all the Psalms in between.

The revelation which emerges in this chapter is not of Jesus, God become man, as in the previous six examples, but rather of Jesus the pre-existent, eternal wisdom of God.[52] Paul and John both understand this designation for Jesus. Paul tells us that Christ is 'God's wisdom'[53] and that 'all treasures of wisdom are hidden in Christ'[54] which seems to reflect the mining imagery of verses 1-11 of the Job 28 hymn. John employs the similar concept of the Eternal Word for Jesus, rather than eternal wisdom, as in John 1:1 'in the beginning was the Word', and 1 John 1:1 'what was from the beginning…the Word of Life'.

Wisdom by Investigation or Revelation

Job chapter 28, 'The Hymn to Wisdom', shows man seeking out wisdom, but despite his ingenuity and technology in digging (mining) for truth, it remains hidden from him. This describes fairly accurately the previous 27 chapters of Job's search for the truth about his suffering circumstances. If wisdom is not 'in the land of the living' (v. 13), where can it be found (v.12)? Where can it come from (v.20)? It appears that God alone understands its 'way' and knows where it is because he worked with wisdom

---

52 cf Matt 11:19 and Luke 7:35 where Jesus identifies himself as the wisdom of God.

53 1 Corinthians 1:24 & 30

54 Colossians 2:3

to create the world (v.23-27). This invokes an idea similar to Proverbs 8:22-31 where wisdom was possessed at the beginning of God's way and was involved with the creation process. No wonder God alone knows wisdom's 'way' since they share the same 'way' from the beginning of God, that is, from eternity. Wisdom is seen as both eternal and personal:

> *Then He (the Creator God) saw it (lit. 'her') and declared*
> *(appraised) it (her); He established (arranged) it (her)*
> *and searched it (her) out.*
> *And to man He said, 'Behold, the fear of the Lord, that is*
> *wisdom; And to depart from evil is understanding.'*
> *(Job 28:27-28)*

Wisdom appears personified as a woman in the book of Proverbs, and is one of the Old Testament anticipations of the Trinitarian God revealed in the New Testament. As we have seen, the imagery is picked up and interpreted as the person of Christ by New Testament writers. Job's hymn sings of 'Eternal Wisdom'. All through chapter 28 'wisdom' has the definite article until these verses 27-28 where Wisdom begins to appear as a personification of God's revelation. Wisdom is a person together with the Father and the Spirit, who is outside all that is created and therefore who holds the truth which can give meaning to everything that happens inside the created order. The same personification comes out even more clearly in Proverbs 8. This Wisdom is the revelation which is essential for finding meaning in the problem of suffering with which Job has been grappling.

So, the six glimpses of Jesus that Job has already seen in his pain and his protests are revelations of the eternal Wisdom of God who, of course, has always been there. That is how he has been able to break through into Job's experience, the steadying rock beneath his feet, even centuries before he would actually break through into time and space in human flesh. Wisdom was revealed to humanity in the person of Jesus Christ, bringing revelation to all the questions of life, including suffering. Human investigation and ingenuity, as seen in the beginning of the Hymn to Wisdom, ultimately can resolve no problem and give no meaning. Only the revelation of Jesus Christ, the eternal Son of the Godhead, can fill the heart of Job with hope, love and purpose in the midst of his despair. We might think today in the terms of John the Apostle, that the Word was made flesh and dwelt amongst us and we beheld his glory as of the only begotten of the Father full of grace and truth[55]. Job's heart glimpsed this eternal truth as he sang his Hymn to Wisdom, 2000 years before it was incarnated, and as he did, he was being led into the Trinitarian God.

---

55 John 1:14

8

Church Streams and Jesus' Ministry

I think it is fascinating to see that each of these aspects of Jesus' ministry, alluded to prophetically in the book of Job as we saw in the previous chapter, relates to a particular church-stream or denomination.[1] Different parts of the church have emphasised different things about our Lord in their theology and practice, and we all have something to learn from and something to contribute to one another. Let's listen to one another, and see what each has to offer.

---

1 I first began to mediate on this phenomenon having read a paper by Goldingay, who comments on most of these denominational theological emphases. I have expanded and adapted his initial comments to fit the six revelations of Jesus in Job as laid out in the previous chapter.

1. Incarnational - Roman Catholic

The Roman Catholics could be seen to be emphasising the *incarnational* God. The Roman Catholic community displays an obvious enthusiasm for the birth of Jesus; there are many traditional pictures of the Christ-child, the baby in the arms of Mary. Of course, sometimes Mary, we think, takes too prominent a place; but Jesus is seen as a true incarnation, with a real mother, having to suckle her breast, and to be brought up by her. Incarnational Theology is particularly Catholic theology. It is the great contribution made and preserved by the Catholic Church.

2. Life and Ministry of Jesus (Didactic/Imitational) – Protestantism & Liberal Protestantism

During the Reformation, people started to grapple with the Bible in a way that had previously been difficult under the Catholicism of the day. This was obviously a good thing, but along with it, the gate was opened to all sorts of sceptical enquiry into the Bible. This was further encouraged by rationalism and the scientific enquiry that developed in the 17th and 18th centuries, where people started asking all sorts of questions about how the universe worked, who we were and where we came from, and so on. They then turned these questions onto the Bible, so that by the 19th century the Bible had come under intense criticism, and was being pulled apart and treated just like any other secular book, even by those who called themselves Christians.

Some of you may already feel disappointed that I suggested the Roman Catholics had something to contribute to church history, but there are also one or two good things that came out of these Liberal Protestant Bible critics! One achievement of their enquiry and criticism of the Bible, was that Jesus was no longer left 'up there in the heavens', sublime and untouchable in his deity, but was 'brought down to earth' where he *really lived the life of a man*. Jesus' historical context and impact was researched, discussed and hotly debated. Of course, Protestantism itself, not just the Liberals, contributed to this, especially in the debates of the early 19th century between Open and Exclusive Brethren and the Catholic Apostolic Church. But the result was that this ineffable, transcendent, unattainable, inaccessible, mediaeval God, who had to be approached through the saints and Mary, was brought down closer and closer to us human beings.

Jesus' real humanity was being rediscovered. Millais' picture of Jesus cutting himself as a boy in the carpenter's shop that I mentioned in the previous chapter was outrageous to people of the day. It made Jesus out to be just like us, it brought Jesus right down to earth. The Times said it was revolting and Charles Dickens deplored it. Of course, once the ground was won for Jesus the man, then the problems arose with reasserting his divinity. Many had made such a case for his humanity that they had lost hold of the fact that he was also God!

However, the benefit, despite the criticism, has been to make it very clear to us that Jesus is as much 'very man' of very man, as he is 'very God of very God'. His humanity is as real as his deity. We have a God whom we know is interested in our human condition, because *he* has been in it! We can say to him, 'We love you, Lord Jesus, because you are one of us.'[2]

As a result, good Protestants ought to be, and are, putting our hands into the problems around us in society, and showing that we are truly human; as much human as our neighbours are. That is what many Christians, not just evangelicals, are doing today, showing that we are concerned for people's humanity. God made it, he wore it, and he loves it. There was a huge explosion in social

---

2   Herman Hesse

action in the 19th century, spearheaded by the Protestant church. This is one particular contribution of Protestantism, and Liberal Protestantism especially. Of course, today Catholic theologians and others also have taken up the social action agenda, and we have all come much closer together.

The Sermon on the Mount

The Liberal Protestant stream has often majored on the teaching of Jesus while he was on earth, living like us. Some would say that the teaching of the Sermon on the Mount ('love your enemies', 'don't worry', 'treat others as you would have them treat you') is all that really matters in Christianity. Social action and good morals are what count; all the complicated stuff about Crucifixion, Resurrection and the Holy Spirit is just confusing the issue.

Well, it is true that the Sermon on the Mount is a wonderful and beautiful piece of teaching. But unless you find the way to live it, you have got problems. We find it, of course, by the work of Jesus in bringing in a New Humanity (not a New Deity). He accomplishes that work by his crucifixion, his resurrection and the pouring out of his Spirit upon us. It is there that we find the power to live the Christian life. The discipling that the apostles were commanded to do[3] is indeed a modelling on the life and lifestyle of Jesus. But Jesus said it began with, 'If anyone wishes to come after Me, let him deny himself, and take up his cross, and follow me'[4] and it finished with 'Receive the Holy Spirit!'[5] Nevertheless, to emphasize following Christ's example and seeking to build our lives on his teaching is a valuable contribution of Protestantism to the Christian church.

3　Matthew 28:18-20

4　Matthew 16:24

5　John 20:22

3. Crucifixional – Evangelical

We preach Christ and him crucified![6] The definition of an evangelical, according to David Bebbington, is: a) we believe that you must be born again and have some definite commitment to our Lord; b) we are activists; c) we take the Bible as our authority; and d) the cross is central to our theology.[7] Crucifixional theology is particularly Evangelical. Evangelicals have not usually majored quite so much on the Sermon on the Mount, as they have upon the blood of the cross. And rightly so, because without the wounds of Jesus for our sins, there is no way for us to be in relationship with God, and thus to draw on his power for holy living.

We are like lamps that cannot work unless we are plugged into the power source. We were never meant to work on our own, and indeed we cannot. But if we plug ourselves into the socket, we are filled with the energy that enables us to function correctly. Without the cross, which is like the socket, we cannot plug ourselves into God; we cannot have fellowship with him. The cross enables us to live in him and he in us, so that we can draw on his divine power to live lives that glorify him, and reflect more of who he is.

Bebbington's second point is that we are activists. We should be, as we saw in the section above, because out of our gratitude to God, out of our joy of being forgiven and knowing his love, we want to run all over the world as missionaries, doing all sorts of social action, and loving and helping people everywhere. Over 90% of the social action of the 19th century was done by evan-

---

6   1 Corinthians 1:23; 2:2

7   Bebbington defines these four key elements as Conversionism, Activism, Biblicism, and Cruicicentrism, in his *Evangelicalism in Modern Britain: A History From the 1730s to the 1980s* (London: Unwin Hyman, 1989), pp. 2-19.

gelical Christians, according to a historian speaking in the Open University textbook, 'The Saints in Politics'.

We are activists because we thank God for what he has done in saving us; giving us a relationship, giving us eternal life. So I shall never stop preaching the cross; in fact, there is no theme like it. I hardly ever preach without somewhere bringing in the cross of our Lord Jesus Christ. It is the most magnificent revelation of the heart of God that we can ever find. We shall go on worshipping around the fact of it all through eternity. For there, on the throne, is the Lamb, 'standing, as slain'[8]. We shall enjoy the crucified God forever, because there is none other worthy of the name 'God' than he. Keeping the Cross central is a right and worthy contribution that evangelicalism has made.

4. Resurrectional – Orthodox

But we must not forget Resurrectional Theology! It may be another surprise to some, but the Eastern Orthodox Church particularly emphasises the resurrection in its theology. On Easter morning in many Eastern cultures, the traditional greeting on the streets for atheists and Christians alike, is: 'Christ is risen!' and the reply: 'He is risen indeed!' That is good Orthodox stuff!

In an Orthodox way of thinking, almost everything is interpreted through the resurrection of Jesus. Take, for example, Genesis 3:15. After the fall of man, the LORD speaks to the serpent about the 'seed' or the 'offspring' of the woman, saying: 'He shall bruise you on the head, and you shall bruise him on the heel.' ('Bruise' is sometimes translated 'strike at' or 'crush'.) We in the West read that and emphasise the cross. It is a prophecy, sometimes called the 'protoeuangelion' — the first gospel — and it comes right at the beginning of the Bible, as soon as man has fallen. Immediately,

---

8   Revelation 5:6

God introduces the gospel of redemption: as Jesus' foot comes down to crush the serpent's head, his heel will be bitten, snapped at—and this is the cross. Christ was bitten, but he crushed Satan as it happened.

But the Orthodox interpretation, just as sincere and positive, is not so focussed on the death of Jesus, but more on the death of the serpent, the one who brought in death! When the serpent dies it signifies 'the death of death'. As Jesus' heel came down, it crushed the head of Satan, who had the power of death; so death is defeated, and the possibility of resurrection life is introduced. It is the killing of the killer that we rejoice over; the bringing of death to the one who brought death. Satan has been defeated. So the final word of that beautiful picture is resurrection: you don't beat death unless you rise again! That is Resurrectional Theology. It is the hope of the Gospel—if Christ is not raised, our faith is in vain[9] —the resurrection of our Lord Jesus. One of my favourite novels comes from the Orthodoxy of Russia. It is Tolstoy's *Resurrection*. The Eastern church has certainly had something important to contribute over the centuries.

5. Ascensional – Charismatic/ Pentecostal

Ascensional Theology has largely risen up in the 20th century. It focuses on the fact that the Lord Jesus has sat down at the right hand of God, and 'having received from the Father the promise of the Holy Spirit, He has poured forth this which you both see and hear'[10]. These are the words Peter addressed to the crowds on the day of Pentecost, when the Holy Spirit was poured out. The outpouring of the Spirit comes from the throne of God, and so it is the evidence that Jesus is enthroned, that he is in the place of all authority and power.

9   I Corinthians 15:14
10 Acts 2:33

Elijah said to Elisha, 'If you see me go up, you shall receive a double-portion of my spirit.'[11] Acts 1 mentions Jesus' being 'taken up' or 'lifted up' four times, before, in chapter 2, the Spirit comes down. If we look up to Jesus, who is exalted and enthroned, we shall receive the promise of the Holy Spirit. We shall know, if we fix our eyes on the Lord Jesus, that it is indeed the Holy Spirit we are receiving, and not something else. That is the basis of Pentecostal/Charismatic theology, which has been a rising influence in the church throughout the last century and into this one. A well known conservative theologian and writer has said, 'Well, every church is a bit Charismatic-y these days isn't it?' If this is true, then partly due to the influence of the Pentecostal and Charismatic church, we have been saved this last century from practical Binitarianism to living Trinitarianism—as we ought always to have been.

6. Eschatological – Universal

I cannot think of any particular denomination or movement which has yet strongly taken up this last point, but I believe its influence is increasing, though not in one denomination, but all. In our lifetime, we have seen many denominational walls and barriers coming down; churches are better at working together and their theologies mix and contribute to one another, thereby often becoming more potent. I believe that there is a theological emphasis rising up that is looking forward to the second coming of Jesus. Scholars and churches are placing more and more emphasis on this dimension, which is often called 'eschatology', meaning the study of 'last things'.

'Ecumenicity' is a bit of a buzz-word today—churches working together and sharing together—and there is a true ecumenicity

---

11 2 Kings 2:9-10

that I hope we shall one day reach, where the church is not 'one' in the sense of a structure, or a world-wide bureaucracy, but it is one church, unified across the world in its love for one another, and its commitment to one another and its vision; in speaking well of one another and praying for one another, giving to and encouraging one another; training each other up and living in the Spirit's oneness. In this context, all the theologies and emphases we have seen will have their place: Incarnational, Didactic, Imitational, Crucifixional, Resurrectional, and Ascensional. But there will also be an emphasis on the coming again of Jesus.

We have strayed from the understanding of the Early Church in Acts, where Peter stands up and says, 'As it was written, "In the last days I will pour out my Spirit"'[12]. It was understood that the church age *is* 'the last days'. We are in the end times; we are in the time of the fulfilment of that prophecy that Peter quotes from Joel. We are meant to be living in the culmination of all things; we are meant to be hastening the day of God[13]. We are meant to be reaching into the powers of the age to come and drawing them into this present age. We are meant to be expressing the oneness for which Jesus prayed in John 17:21, and then accomplished and established for us on the cross. That oneness was to be the ground whereby 'the world may believe'[14], and upon which the Holy Spirit will work in all the world to bring the Good News to every tribe, tongue, people and nation. This gospel would be preached in all the world and then the end will come![15]

The church is meant to be *so* burning with love and passion for Jesus that he would not be able to remain in heaven, but being

---

12 Acts 2:17
13 2 Peter 3:11-12
14 John 17:21-23
15 Matthew 24:14

drawn like a magnet, or a comet that started its journey 2,000 years ago, he is on track and coming closer; he is being drawn by our gravity, by the magnetism of love, getting faster and faster as we pull him to the earth. Then suddenly the Lord will appear! That is dynamic, eschatological, last-days theology that began with Peter in Acts 2, and has begun to have an emphasis in the church once again.

So maybe all these six theologies we have looked at, as they come together and balance one another out, will help us to stand in 'end time theology' - and we shall see the end come and the Lord return. Are you ready for it? That is what we are after! Let us therefore 'hasten the day'![16]

---

16 2 Peter 3:11-12

9

Kinsman-Redeemer

Now we come to look more closely at one of the central reasons for Job's suffering. Let us remind ourselves of Job 19:25, those famous words:

> *And as for me, I know that my Redeemer lives,*
> *And at the last He will take His stand on the earth.*

The word 'Redeemer' is *Ga'al* in the Hebrew.[1] It refers to 'a relative who redeems'. Since there were no police forces and not so many law courts around in the ancient world, people under pressure relied on a member of the family, one who was as closely related as possible, to look after their interests. Whether they liked

---

1 *Ga'al* is pronounced 'go-el'. See the Book of Ruth for a beautiful account of a kinsman-redeemer.

you or not did not matter, they were honour-bound to help you if you appealed to them under the 'kinsman-redeemer' accepted code of conduct.

For example, if you became suddenly poverty-stricken and had to sell your property, it was the duty of the kinsman-redeemer to de-mortgage it for you. If you could not pay your debts and were taken off as a slave, the kinsman-redeemer would have to pay the price to buy back your freedom. If somebody murdered you, your kinsman-redeemer would have to make sure that justice was done by tracking down the murderer and finishing him off. That was the job of a *ga'al*. They were completely and utterly committed to you and to your interests.

Who is our kinsman-redeemer, as Christians today? Who is our 'closest relative'? It is the Lord Jesus Christ. He has become our 'close relative' because he became *man*. He has become one of us. He is our elder brother[2], our friend[3] and our neighbour; Jesus is *close* to us, dwelling amongst us as Emmanuel, 'God with us.'[4] As our Kinsman-Redeemer, Jesus has looked after our rights: he has dealt with our sins, our debts: he has defeated the devil and bought us out of slavery into freedom, for 'where the Spirit of the Lord is, there is liberty.'[5] Jean Ingelow puts it so well in the hymn that we began quoting earlier:

> *And didst Thou love the race that loved not Thee?*
> *And didst Thou take to Heaven a human brow?*
> *Dost plead with man's voice by the marvellous sea?*
> *Art Thou his Kinsman now?*

---

2 Romans 8:29
3 John 15:15
4 Matthew 1:23
5 2 Corinthians 3:17

O God, O Kinsman loved, but not enough,
O Man, with eyes majestic after death,
Whose feet have toiled along our pathways rough,
Whose lips drawn human breath!

By that one likeness which is ours and Thine,
By that one nature which doth hold us kin,
By that high Heaven where, sinless,
Thou dost shine To draw us sinners in;

By Thy last silence in the judgment hall,
By long foreknowledge of the deadly tree,
By darkness, by the wormwood and the gall,
I pray Thee visit me.

Come, lest this heart should, cold and cast away,
Die ere the Guest adored she entertain—
Lest eyes which never saw Thine earthly day
Should miss Thy heavenly reign.[6]

What a beautiful expression of the kinsman-redeemer relationship that Jesus has with us!

But here is the crux of the matter: if Jesus is our nearest kinsman, *whose kinsman does that make us?* Well, we must be his! If he is our nearest relative, then necessarily we, the church, are his. Thus, if Jesus has looked after our interests, as near-kinsmen we are here to look after his. That is part of the problem that Job is going through! He is not suffering for correction; he is not suffering because he is a sinner; he is not suffering in order to be taught a lesson; he is not suffering to be made humble. *He is suffering because he is the kinsman of God.* As the kinsman of God, Job was standing to vindicate God and his love in a world that was rejecting God under the influence of Satan. Satan appears for us

6   Jean Ingelow, Poems, 1863.

at the beginning of this book, and will appear again at the end, to show us that he is at war with God. And God has been calling upon his kinsmen—his people, his church—to stand with the Heavenly Kinsman, who has done *everything* for us, and declare that a God like that is worth having, even worth suffering for. That is the calling of the Church of God. Are you willing for it?

We are to vindicate God in the eyes of the world and the devil. We are to prove that God is worth standing for *even if we get nothing out of it*. We are to show that a God of love is worth living and dying for. In chapters 1 and 2 of Job, we saw how Satan accused both God and man: is God only worth loving because he gives good gifts to people who love him? Can a man love God if he gets nothing out of it? Is 'love' really just a selfish emotion disguised as something noble? Job, by his righteous suffering, stood up in the law courts of this universe and declared, 'God is worth loving even if I get nothing out of it!' And the devil was proved wrong. By the end of the book he has nothing more to say! God did not have to smite him out of his courts; he retreated! He was outmanoeuvred with logic and love and reason, there was no ground for him to stand in those courts any longer. And since our Advocate has spoken for us, since our Redeemer has paid the price and stood for us, so now, should we not follow Job and be willing to stand for him?

That is why Job was suffering. We know, because we could read and understand the backdrop to his story in chapters 1 and 2. Job, however, did not know that that is what he was doing. Nevertheless, through those moments of illumination, when he was at his greatest point of pain and suffering, he began to see the sort of God that he needed. His final word about that God was: he is my Kinsman-Redeemer! And therefore, all Job's suffering was an opportunity to be God's *ga'al* in return, to stand for God's interests when he was under attack.

Much of the suffering that goes on in the world is a result of the enemy's spite. It is his strategy to try and bring our God down, malign his character, and destroy the work he is doing with men and women in bringing in his kingdom life. When we suffer like this, we are engaging in the battle. Once we have searched, and asked the Lord to search our hearts, and made sure that it is not our own sin that causes us to suffer, then we may well conclude that we are in the same position as Job. So, when we are under pressure, when our souls are crushed, when our bodies are being attacked, and we cry out to the Lord for grace and help, let us do so in the knowledge that he is our redeemer, *and we are his:* let us declare that we will stand with him forever.

No matter what theological persuasion you come from, whether you agree with my analysis here or not, we cannot deny that endurance is a fundamental Christian principle, and we find it all over the New Testament.[7] We must never give up. We must never stop standing for the Lord. We must never stop defending his love. 'Though he slay us, we will hope in him!' It was not God slaying Job, it was the devil. But even though he couldn't understand all that he was going through, he still trusted God, to the end. That is the kind of Church that God is looking for. Sadly, we often want to be a church that only receives blessings and good things, but is never prepared to stand against the bad. It takes determination, perseverance and endurance to suffer as Job did. But if we do, the rewards are sweet. It was for the joy set before him that Christ endured the cross.[8] The reward of his sufferings was to receive us into his family and enjoy close communion with us, his people, for eternity.

Job was not suffering all his life. Nor did Jesus suffer outwardly, as he did on the cross, all his life. Standing firm under

---

7   John 16:33; Ephesians 6:13; Hebrews 10:35-39

8   Hebrews 12:2

suffering as a vindication of the Lord is for a time, or a season, in our experience. The apostle Paul told us, 'all who desire to live godly in Christ Jesus will be persecuted'[9]. If we are seeking to follow Jesus, we should not be too surprised when these kinds of attacks arise. Sometimes they may spring up unexpectedly and knock us off our feet; then we have to stand up again. But this is not to say that the Christian life is nothing but a misery and under continual persecution. We should not expect to be suffering all the time. There were times when Jesus 'rejoiced greatly in the Holy Spirit'[10] when he saw what God was doing; how he was moving towards the great climax of the work that would bring the world back into relationship with God. That was the great joy that the Father, Son and Spirit were working for during Jesus' mission here on earth. There is joy and there is triumph in this life; but there are also those times when we experience the heat of the frontline in the battlefield. Soldiers are not all on the frontline, all of the time. In fact, very few are there at any one time, and not for very long. They get called back again, to safer ground to have a good rest, before they go out again to have another go at the enemy.

This is the way in which we must understand the particular sort of suffering that Job was going through. It was a kind of spiritual warfare. It was a suffering which was *bringing a vindication to God;* justifying God. It was showing the world and the powers of the universe that he is the best. It was engaging with what theologians call the problem of theodicy (God's justice). It was showing that there is an answer to that problem, if we will hear it; but it involves us valuing the love of God, as demonstrated in Christ Jesus, so much that we are willing to keep loving him in return, even if we get nothing out of it. That is the kind of love

---

9   2 Timothy 3:12

10   Luke 10:21

that took Jesus to the Cross, even for his enemies and those that betrayed him. And if we want to be sharers in his divine nature, thus revealed, that is the only way, ultimately, in which we too are meant to live.

> *This is the God whom I adore,*
> *My faithful, unchangeable friend;*
> *His love is as strong as his power,*
> *And neither knows measure nor end.*

10

The Revelation of God to Suffering

Then the LORD answered Job...
(Job 38:1; 40:6)

We come now to God's answer to Job's complaints in the last five chapters of the book, Job 38-42. He gives two replies, two fundamental pieces of revelation, to show Job how suffering comes to be, and why it took place in him. The first answer starts in 38:1 with the words, 'Then the Lord answered Job out of the whirlwind and said...' The second answer begins in 40:6, 'Then the Lord answered Job out of the storm and said...' God breaks in twice, with a whirlwind and with a storm, and each answer has a different emphasis.

The answer from the whirlwind aims to make Job understand that the universe is extremely complex. 'Understanding' is the key concept. This section, 38:1-40:5, starts and ends with the word, acting like brackets, or signposts, standing near the beginning and the end, to draw your attention to what is in the middle.

> *Where were you when I laid the foundation of the earth?*
> *Tell Me, if you have understanding (Job 38:4)...*

> *...Is it by your understanding that the hawk soars,*
> *Stretching his wings toward the south? (Job 39:26)*

God is explaining to Job that he does not have total understanding. The universe is an extremely deep and complex entity. Job does not have all the facts at his disposal in order to solve the conundrum of why he should be suffering. God is *not* saying, therefore, that Job (or you or I) can never have a clue as to why it is that we suffer. He is just saying that this is one of the factors that we must keep in mind when we get frustrated and think there are no answers to the deep questions of life.

The things that God brings to Job to show him the wonder and complexity of the whole created order may not impress us so much today. We have discovered so much more about the world we inhabit since those ancient times! But we still do not understand everything. If God were speaking to us today, rather than using ostriches and mountain goats, as he does with Job, perhaps he would talk in terms of the indeterminacy of particles, or throw in a bit of quantum physics, or refer us to some distant galaxy. The message is still the same: it is a complex universe, and we need God to break in from outside to give us understanding of it. The universe is simply not set up to allow us to live a 'do-it-yourself' life!

God's second answer, the answer from the storm, starting at Job 40:6, concerns the powers of evil and chaos. There is a short introduction to this answer in 40:6-14, and then it divides into two parts. The first part talks of the creature 'Behemoth'[1], and the second part is about the creature 'Leviathan'[2]. Thomas Aquinas understood these creatures simplistically as the elephant and the whale. Sometimes they have been called, slightly more sophisticatedly, the hippopotamus and the crocodile. But these readings have been foisted onto the text as people have tried to fit the names to animals with which we are familiar. That is not what was intended by the writer. These creatures, these bits of God's creation, leave us perplexed precisely because they symbolise cosmic spiritual forces, such as we have already been introduced to in Job 1 and 2. Perhaps by this point in the story, after so much more human affairs have dominated the plot with complaints and arguments, we have forgotten the spiritual powers that first set the scene for us. But Satan reappears in this last part of the book, symbolised by these strange creatures, Behemoth and Leviathan, just as he appeared as a serpent in Genesis, in the garden of Eden.

Rather than searching for our own human explanations of these creatures, we need to understand God's perspective on them. We shall look carefully into the Scripture concerning Leviathan, the seven-headed monster, who reappears in the Book of Revelation, along with a beast from the sea, whom we can understand to be Behemoth. As we look at these, and other verses, we shall get a fuller view of how Scripture uses these creatures to show us negative supernatural powers, which are brought under control only by God.

Unless God breaks in and brings revelation, as he does here to Job in the whirlwind and the storm, then there is no solution to the great enigmas of the universe. We cannot know who God is and how he runs the show unless he tells us. It is too complicated

---

1   Job 40:15-24

2   Job 41

and too supernatural for us to understand it all fully without help. If I choose not to reveal myself to you, you will not fully know me. God is not any less than us; he is greater! If he did not want to speak to us and show himself to us, he would not. But he has—we know who God is, because he has spoken to us in Christ[3]! He has revealed himself in Jesus. 'If you have seen me,' says Jesus, 'you have seen the Father'[4]. Without revelation there is no knowing of God, nor of the intricacies of how he created this universe to run, and why. We need revelation, if we are ever going to get any answers at all. Human investigation alone will not do it. In this, at least, Zophar was right when he said: 'Can you by searching find out God?'[5]

Answer from the Whirlwind—The Complexity of the Universe (Job 38:1-40:5)

> *Then the Lord answered Job out of the whirlwind and said,*
> *'Who is this that darkens counsel*
> *By words without knowledge?*
> *Now gird up your loins like a man,*
> *And I will ask you, and you instruct Me! (Job 38:1-3)*

Job's ardent and persistent desire to speak with God, and to hear what the LORD has to say about his plight is finally answered. Elihu hinted that God might appear in a dramatic fashion in the beautiful poetry of chapter 37 'Listen closely to the thunder of His voice…Under the whole heaven He lets it loose, and His lightning to the ends of the earth. After it, a voice roars; He thunders with His majestic voice…[6] Elijah was caught up to heaven in a

---

3   Hebrews 1:1
4   John 14:9
5   Job 11:7 KJV
6   Job 37:2-4

whirlwind[7], so it seems it is a means by which God likes to make his presence felt!

Stand up and be a man

The first thing that God says may surprise us. 'Gird up your loins like a man.' There are situations we will face in life where we have to stand up and 'be a man', or 'be a woman'. We have to gird up our loins and look things in the face – sometimes, look God in the face. Our affluent, self-indulgent 21st century lifestyle sadly produces human beings who expect everything to be easy and comfortable, and who, when it is not, slip easily into misery, wretchedness and self-pity. Like lumps of putty, we have become the passive victims of every experience that comes our way and promises instant relief from our wretchedness, never taking the trouble to stop and question it, to evaluate what is soaking into our lives and whether it will do us any long term good. It means that most of the time we are not acting like men or women, we are behaving more like children. Men and women are made in the image of God. God wants us to make choices and decisions that will be productive in our lives. He urges us to overcome sin and evil when it seeks to overtake us.[8] Peter tells us to (literally) 'gird up the loins of our mind'[9] - prepare our minds for action, get ready to think godly thoughts and make godly choices!

If we honour God we will play the man, we will play the woman when the chips are down. We will stand up, gird up our loins, and look things in the face. Even if we are suffering, we will not indulge in self-pity. We will ask God what we should do, and we

---

7   Not in a chariot! The chariot remained and reappears later with a few others. cf 2 Kings 2:1 & 11; 6:17).

8   Genesis 4:6-7

9   1 Peter 1:13

will find that he might say, 'I will show you what things you must suffer for My name's sake.'[10] That is what he said to the apostle Paul. I wish it could be different sometimes! I wish God would say, 'I will show you what great things you shall indulge in for My sake! You shall be so blessed up and it will be such a lovely time for you, you won't know what's hit you!' That is often the way the Gospel is preached these days. And of course we know we shall be blessed! We can hardly be in God's presence without being so! But his blessings are not to indulge us, like some pathetically spineless person who never has to make hard choices and face things for themselves. Self-pity is the greatest paralysis that will stop you from doing anything useful for God. When you feel sorry for yourself, you do not do anything; you want everybody else to do something for you. Stand up! Be a man! Be a woman! Gird up your loins!

Then God starts to be slightly sarcastic with Job. 'Where were you when I laid the foundation of the earth? Tell Me, if you have understanding...'[11] God is pointing out that from the way Job has been talking, he must have been there at the beginning. If he expects to know everything without being told, he must have seen how God formed everything, and understand the majestic intricacies of this huge, wonderful, complicated universe! God continues: 'Who set its measurements, since you know?'[12] So Job starts to think: 'Ah, well—no, I wasn't actually there at the time...' We might think it slightly unfair of God to be sarcastic, after all Job has been through. But God does not indulge Job in his self-pity; he talks to Job in such a way as to pull him up, help him to snap out of it and be ready to stand on his feet and face the truth. And what a wonderful revelation of truth he turns out to receive!

10 Acts 9:15
11 Job 38:4
12 Job 38:5a

Sons of God

> *Or who laid its cornerstone [the earth's],*
> *When the morning stars sang together,*
> *And all the sons of God shouted for joy? (Job 38:6b-7)*

The 'sons of God' first appeared in Job chapters 1 and 2, and now here, in the final chapters of the book, they appear again. God's revelation to Job at the end of the book picks up on several of the spiritual things to which we were introduced at the beginning. The cosmic backdrop to Job's story, of which we as the readers were aware all along, is finally beginning to be made known to Job. When God created the universe, he made the heavenly beings before he made the earthly ones. That is why Genesis 1:1 says that in the beginning God created the heavens—and presumably filled them up—and *then* the earth; and we go on to read the six day account of how he filled that up.

When God created the earth, at first it was 'without form and empty'[13]. There was a great sea of formlessness and emptiness, which is called 'the deep'. Then the Spirit of God moves upon it, and God begins to form it and fill it. He first moulds the chaos and the randomness into forms, and then he fills those forms.

We read about the forming process in the first three days of creation in Genesis 1. The first form was light/darkness or day/night. The second form was waters above/waters below. The third form was earth/sea. Thus, God was forming the 'deep chaos' which had been without form. He was beginning to bring order out of chaos, by creating distinctions defined by the power of his Word. The Word of God brings distinctions, differences and definitions to our experience of the universe to stop it being a chaotic, meaningless mass. The Word of God says 'that is a man' and 'that is a

---

13 Genesis 1:2

woman'; he does not say that they are the same thing, or that we can interact with them how we like. The Word of God tells us what things are and how to relate to them, not our genetics, nor what we happen to feel, nor our psychology. It is God who declares it. God said, 'this is day' and 'this is night', and he brought these distinctions by his Word.

But the earth was not just 'without form', it was 'empty'. In the next three days, we read about how the 'forms' were 'filled'. God fills the heavens of day and night with sun, moon and stars. He fills the seas of the 'waters below' with monsters and fish, and the skies of the 'waters above' with 'every winged bird'; and the whole place is said to be teeming and swarming with living creatures. Then, on the sixth day, he puts animals on the dry land of the earth, and finally he 'created man in his own image'.

God formed and filled out of the formlessness and emptiness. So, if he formed and filled the earth when he created it, we assume he had already formed and filled the heavens, the spiritual realms, when he created them. Thus we read that 'the sons of God shouted for joy'[14] at the laying of the earth's foundation. It must have been a wonderful day; the morning stars singing, the sons of God shouting for joy![15] Why were they so happy? Because the harmony which was going to be created from this inharmonious random matter, was the harmony that they already enjoyed. They had already been formed, filled and ordered; they had structures of principalities, powers, dominions, thrones and hosts of angels. So when they see more order created from chaos in the earthly realms, they get rather happy about it! The matter of earth reflects the harmony of heaven as God breathes his creative Word into it.

---

14 Job 38:6-7

15 'Morning Stars' and 'Sons of God' are a hendiadys – they both refer to the same thing: the 'heavenly beings'.

Proverbs 8:22-31 declares that Wisdom, Jesus, was with God at the foundation of the heavens and the earth, and John 1:3 reveals that 'all things came into being by Him', that is Jesus, the Word. In Genesis 1:2, the Spirit or the 'Breath' of God was brooding over the waters at creation, so that God and his Word and his Breath were working altogether in unison when the world was founded.

These brief references to the spiritual realms, which teem with life at least as much as our earthly realms do, give us glimpses into the vast complexities of how God handles the thousands of wills that interact in the universe he has created. So God mentions them now, to Job, as part of the answer to his experience of suffering.

The Natural World (Job 38:4-38)

God's answer to Job from the whirlwind divides nicely into two parts: first, God shows Job the world of nature in Job 38:4-38, and then, the world of animals in Job 38:39-39:30. Both contain complexities that are beyond the capabilities of man to fully fathom.

> *First, the sea: Or who enclosed the sea with doors,*
> *When, bursting forth, it went out from the womb;*
> *When I made a cloud its garment,*
> *And thick darkness its swaddling band,*
> *And I placed boundaries on it,*
> *And I set a bolt and doors,*
> *And I said, 'Thus far you shall come, but no farther;*
> *And here shall your proud waves stop'? (Job 38:8-11)*

The seas are pictured like an unruly child, bursting forth from the womb. They need the control and discipline of God: 'So far, no further!' Can man work out how to handle the sea? Thousands of years later we haven't managed it yet!

Next, the morning; can man cause the sun to rise? And then a passage describing the underworld, the place of the departed using ancient imagery:

> *Have you entered into the springs of the sea?*
> *Or have you walked in the recesses of the deep?*
> *Have the gates of death been revealed to you?*
> *Or have you seen the gates of deep darkness?*
> *Have you understood the expanse of the earth?*
> *Tell Me, if you know all this. (Job 38:16-18)*

Man cannot plunder the mysteries of death in this life; they are too far away, on the other side of the grave. It is the Lord who determines what happens in Sheol, who orders the place of the departed.

Next God draws our attention to the elements: the 'storehouses of the snow and the hail', the 'channel for the flood', or the 'way for the thunderbolt', 'rain, dew, ice and frost'. Is man the author of these changes in the weather?

Now we turn to the stars:

> *Can you bind the chains of the Pleiades,*
> *Or loose the cords of Orion?*
> *Can you lead forth a constellation in its season,*
> *And guide the Bear with her satellites?*
> *Do you know the ordinances of the heavens,*
> *Or fix their rule over the earth? (Job 38:31-33)*

Does man hold the 'chains' and the 'cords' that cause the stars to move in harmony and keep in the order of their orbits? Surely that is God's domain; what can man know of the stars?

The final references in this section on the natural world is to the 'innermost being' and the 'mind'.[16] These do not seem to quite fit in the same category with the other inanimate images of the sea and the underworld and the dawn. However, the word for 'innermost being' is probably better translated as 'ibis'[17], and the word for 'mind' as 'cockerel'[18] (as the NJB and the TEV have it), which would give us:

> *Who has put wisdom in the ibis,*
> *Or has given understanding to the cockerel?*

Although these two birds are not inanimate either, they do fit with the theme of the preceding section because the ibis is said to announce a change of weather, and of course the cockerel is known to herald the dawn. Where do they get their wisdom from? Certainly not from man, who takes his cue from the song of these birds! It is the Lord who has created a universe that moves and changes by the pattern he has fixed.

These are the mysteries of the inanimate world that still amaze us and cause us to worship in even our sophisticated society today!

The animal world (Job 38:39-39:30)

Now God moves on to the complexities of the animal kingdom.

> *Can you hunt the prey for the lion,*
> *Or satisfy the appetite of the young lions?...*
> *...Who prepares for the raven its nourishment*
> *When its young cry to God? (Job 38:39-41)*

---

16 Job 38:36

17 Hebrew word *tuchot*

18 Hebrew word *sekwi*

Man does not know how to provide for these ravenous creatures
– he probably spent a lot of time in the ancient world avoiding
being their next meal, let alone worrying about hunting for them.
It is God who orders the food chain and makes sure his creatures
do not go hungry.

> *Do you know the time the mountain goats give birth?*
> *(Job 39:1)*

There are many things that happen in the animal world that we
humans do not take much notice of. But God takes notice. He is
responsible for the mountain goats and he marks the date when
they are due to give birth, so he'll be sure not to miss it!

Job 39:5-8 compares the wild donkey to the domesticated one.

> *He scorns the tumult of the city,*
> *The shoutings of the driver he does not hear. (Job 39:7)*

His domesticated cousin may be brought under these strictures,
but not this wild donkey; he is going to do his own thing! On the
surface, who can tell the difference between two donkeys? Man
may not be able to, but God can, for he created the unique disposi-
tion of each.

So God goes on to talk of the wild ox, the ostrich, and the horse,
and finishes up in verses 26-30 with the hawk and the eagle:

> *Is it by your understanding that the hawk soars,*
> *stretching his wings toward the south? (Job 39:26)*

These chapters are a beautiful piece of poetry, and as you read
them you can spend time enjoying and laughing at the colourful
pictures God paints of his own creation of which he is so evi-
dently proud and delights to show it off to Job.

Playing God

All these complex entities of the natural and animal world function according to the forming and the filling of God. They came into being as God created things from out of that deep chaos that was otherwise untameable. If you are thinking of running the world, you have a big job on your hands! There are six billion people praying different prayers to cope with for a start—three billion for rain and three billion for sunshine!—but on top of that, you have ostriches screeching out, wild oxen with their demands, and lions making a noise about where they are getting their next meal from; you have a terrifically intricate and complicated universe to keep going.

That is the job that God has in maintaining this universe moment by moment—like a television set. Not only has he switched it on, he is also like the power source, keeping the whole show running every single moment of every day. Adam wanted to be God. He wanted the tree of the knowledge of good and evil; in other words, to be able to say, 'I am the final criterion of what is right and what is wrong.' He started playing God. But when we start, we have a problem. The world is simply too big for little scraps of dust like us to manage.

Complexity and confusion of battle

We tend to want the universe to be neat and tidy, but it is not. If we thought cutting one problematic bit out of the picture might help neaten things up a bit, we would probably find the whole thing would collapse, because every little bit of it is intricately linked and inter-dependant. Similarly, the war in which we are engaged is not as simplistic as: 'you are a good person, you will be blessed; you are a bad person, you won't.' Sadly, people get hit indiscriminately with the shrapnel of the attacks. Good things happen to bad people and bad things to the good. The war in which we are engaged is as messy and as complicated as the universe in which we live.

There is a randomness to the cosmic battle that Satan is waging against God, and this is often what causes us to question 'why?' when we get hit. In part, it is random because Satan and his forces are not omnipresent – they cannot be everywhere at once. If they were, maybe Satan would exercise his warfare with more universal order and predictability. The truth is he just has to take up what opportunities he can lay his hands on. Nor is Satan omniscient. He cannot see or know everything all the time, and this sometimes adds to the randomness of his attacks. He may be aiming at somebody else, but you got hit on the way, like the crossfire in a battle. Real battles are extremely complex; and this is a real battle, not a fairground game, set up so that the children are all safe, where everybody stands back behind the line as the shots are aimed directly at the target. There is confusion as Satan employs any means possible to bring God down. Yet in the midst of the confusion, when we are caught in the crossfire, the suffering we experience can feel very deliberate and personal. We either blame God or the devil for picking on us, when often it was neither. It was just random acts of evil that caught you a blow.

Of course, as we have seen, this analysis does not apply to Job's particular experience of suffering. The devil was picking on him, and it was personal. But overall, in general and for the most part, suffering hits randomly. Sometimes we suffer and somebody else does not. It is not because we were particularly bad or wicked, or even that we were particularly good. Those sorts of things will always happen in a battle. Until the whole of this universe is brought back under God's order, we shall find things happening that are difficult to understand. If we have the battle worldview, we can understand that people suffer, but not always why this one suffers and that one does not.

Honour Those Who Suffer

Every year on Remembrance Sunday we wear poppies to remember those who gave their lives for us in the two World Wars. We honour their memory. Today, in church life, it is not unusual to hear such attitudes as 'That person is suffering, they must be secretly sinning!' or 'That person would be relieved of their suffering if they had a stronger faith!' Christians are so often humiliated, put down, ignored or overlooked when they suffer. But we should honour those who are victims of the spiritual battle we face. In warfare, it is usual to honour the victims, and even at times ascribe them more glory than the heroes who won great victories. Let us not do any less for the victims of our spiritual warfare.

Neither should we try to find some mysterious reason why this one suffered and that one did not. We would never do that in an earthly war. That is a terribly wrong approach to the great complexity of battle. Some of us will know what it is to have lost friends through a disaster that was somebody else's fault, while we missed that same disaster by inches. It would be wrong to dishonour those who fell by trying to find a spiritual reason for our own survival. It sets ourselves forward as somehow more important: 'God must have something more important for me to do, whereas that poor fellow was just worthless.' Those kinds of attitudes exist because there is a misunderstanding of the sort of universe in which we live. The complexity of it makes it impossible to give a reason for every single specific thing that happens.

All kingdoms, including God's, are established and run with a complex infrastructure. In the battle that rages against God's kingdom, sometimes we are hit and sometimes we are not; sometimes somebody else is being aimed at, but we get hit en route; children sometimes get hurt because their parents were being aimed at. It is sad, but we will never resolve all the whys this side of eternity. However, that does not mean that we resignedly say, 'How tragic! But God moves in mysterious ways…' It is not that kind of mystery. God is not being deliberately mysterious to us, rather, the mystery lies in this universe, the battle and the way that the devil is shooting; that is what is so complicated; and we get caught in the crossfire. I am not giving you a simple answer to suffering, because it is not a simple matter. This is what we realise when we listen to God's answer to Job.

> *Then Job answered the Lord and said,*
> *'Behold, I am insignificant; what can I reply to You?*
> *I lay my hand on my mouth.*
> *Once I have spoken, and I will not answer;*
> *Even twice, and I will add no more.' (Job 40:3-5)*

Job responds to admit that he was not there at the creation of this complex universe. He is awed at the greatness of what God has created, and realises that he does not understand it all; so he will be quiet for a while and listen!

Answer from the Storm—Chaos and the Powers of Evil (Job 40:6-41:34)

> *Then the Lord answered Job out of the storm, and said,*
> *'Now gird up your loins like a man;*
> *I will ask you, and you instruct Me.' (Job 40:6-7)*

Thus begins the second part of God's answer to Job. Once again the challenge to Job is 'gird up your loins like a man' - face the issues! Then God gently pokes fun at Job:

> *Adorn yourself with eminence and dignity;*
> *And clothe yourself with honor and majesty.*
> *Pour out the overflowings of your anger;*
> *And look on everyone who is proud, and make him low.*

> *...Then I will also confess to you,*
> *That your own right hand can save you.*
> *(Job 40:10, 11, 14)*

In other words, 'Put on your kingly robes, Job, since you sound like you're the one in charge of everything!' If Job can prove he really does know how best things should run, then God will step aside and let him wield his 'power' to change the universe and save himself. But as we shall see, Job is ill-equipped to save himself, or anyone else for that matter, from the forces that are behind his suffering.

The second reason for Job's suffering also falls into two parts. One focuses on the creature Behemoth, the other on Leviathan.

Behemoth, 'First of God's ways' (Job 40:15-24)

Behemoth is the first of the two creatures; strange creatures with strange names. It is almost impossible to satisfactorily identify them with any particular animal. Some have tried to identify Behemoth with the hippopotamus, and thus you will find him in the margin of some Bibles. But that idea is best left in the margin, (if it is possible to do that with a hippopotamus), for look how he is described in verse 19:

> *He is the first of the ways of God...*

Did God make the hippopotamus first? You could build some interesting theology around that! No, of course not. We have already seen that the first thing that God began to deal with at creation was the chaotic 'deep', the sea; that mysterious entity which is in disarray and needs to be formed and filled. For Behemoth to be called the 'first of the ways of God' must mean that he was around before anything else. He cannot therefore be a normal animal, because God created all sorts of other things before he got to the animals on day six.

Behemoth, the 'first of the ways of God' must be a supernatural creature who exists in this area of chaos that lies at the basis of creation. He is seen to be at war with his maker, fighting against God's order:

Let his maker bring near his sword. (Job 40:19b)

Leviathan, 'King over all the Sons of Pride' (Job 41)

Leviathan cannot be a literal animal either. His description makes him sound more like a mythical dragon than a crocodile:

His sneezes flash forth light,
And his eyes are like the eyelids of the morning.
Out of his mouth go burning torches;
Sparks of fire leap forth. (Job 41:18-19)

Verse 15 talks about his 'strong scales', which are 'his pride', and then in verse 34 it says:

He looks on everything that is high;
He is king over all the sons of pride.

Wherever there is *pride*, this creature reigns. He has been given jurisdiction over 'the sons of pride'; his kingdom exists in every bit of pride. We read that there is nothing 'earthly' about him, and that he is 'one made without fear'[19]. God made the animals to fear man; man was to have dominion over them[20]. But this is no ordinary animal; a creature, yes, but one which is untameable:

Can you put a rope in his nose?...
Will you play with him as with a bird?
Or will you bind him for your maidens? (Job 41:2a, 5)

---

19 Job 41:33
20 Genesis 1:28

Satan in the Book of Job

When the devil, 'the angel of light',[21] this 'Satan' who we read about in the beginning of Job, came into the garden of Genesis 3, he came as a serpent. He came as a beast of the field. Man should have taken authority over him as one of these beasts over whom God had given him dominion. But instead, by obeying him, man gave the devil more authority on the earth. Here at the end of the book of Job Satan appears to us in terms similar to that of Genesis 3, only by now, the snake has grown in horror beyond that of an ordinary snake. Many commentators think that Satan disappears from the story of Job after chapter 2, never to be seen again, and that he is therefore largely irrelevant to the story. In actual fact, we do see him again. We see him in the form of Leviathan, presented before Job in such a way that we begin to see that Satan often tries to disguise himself as a subservient animal. He appears in the garden as a common or garden snake (albeit a talking one!); here in Job, he looks like a big water snake, or an ancient monster; however, when we get to the book of Revelation he is completely unveiled.

Book of Revelation

> *And there was war in heaven, Michael and his angels waging war with the dragon. And the dragon and his angels waged war, and they were not strong enough, and there was no longer a place found for them in heaven. (Revelation 12:7-8)*

Why call him 'the dragon'? Why not just identify him as the devil straight away? Because the picture of a dragon evokes a similar picture to the one we find in Job, and his horrific scaly body and fire-breathing nose express something of the nature of this super-natural being.

21 2 Corinthians 11:14

> *And the great dragon was thrown down, the serpent of*
> *old who is called the devil and Satan, who deceives the*
> *whole world; he was thrown down to the earth, and his*
> *angels were thrown down with him. (Revelation 12:9)*

Satan is unmasked as 'the serpent of old'—the original serpent.[22]
He is that ancient serpent who crept into the garden, 'who is called
the devil and Satan', the adversary and the arch opponent 'who
deceives the whole world'.

'Leviathan' through the Old Testament and in Revelation

As we read on in Revelation 12, we see the words 'dragon' and
'serpent' used interchangeably. In verse 15 'the *serpent*' pours
out water 'like a river out of his mouth'; the next verse says that
the earth 'drank up the river which the *dragon* poured out of its
mouth'. A few verses on, in Revelation 13:4, 'and they worshipped the dragon, because he gave his authority to the beast;…
saying, "Who is like the beast…?"' Who is the beast like? He is
like Leviathan.

> *I saw a beast coming up out of the sea, having ten horns*
> *and seven heads, and on his horns were ten diadems, and*
> *on his heads were blasphemous names.*
> *(Revelation 13:1)*

Leviathan was an ancient mythical monster with seven heads.
Both Satan and the beast are presented to us in the book of Revelation as Leviathan. Revelation 12:3 describes those seven heads
as 'like a dragon's'. They represent the devil, the 'accuser' and

---

22 The NJB has 'the primeval serpent', and other versions 'the ancient
    serpent'.

the 'blasphemer'[23], and Satan, the 'adversary'[24]. All these names, pictures and ideas are rolled together in this embodiment of evil and sin, Satan.

He also appears in the book of Isaiah:

> *In that day the Lord will punish Leviathan the fleeing serpent,*
> *With His fierce and great and mighty sword,*
> *Even Leviathan the twisted serpent;*
> *And He will kill the dragon who lives in the sea. (Isaiah 27:1)*

Here, Leviathan is associated with the sea, just as he is in Revelation 13:1. Satan, as the Beast, emerges from the sea, which Genesis 1 represents to us as a sea of chaos. In Revelation 22:1, the final victory over Satan and Chaos is declared in: 'There was no longer any sea'.

'Leviathan', 'the serpent', 'the dragon', are Old Testament ways of trying to describe this power of evil that is at war with God. We find him in the Psalms too:

> *Yet God is my king from of old,*
> *Who works deeds of deliverance in the midst of the earth.*
> *You divided the sea by Thy strength;*
> *You broke the heads of the sea monsters in the waters.*
> *You crushed the heads of Leviathan;*
> *You gave him as food for the creatures of the wilderness.*
> *(Psalm 74:12-14)*

Notice the plural in verse 14, 'the heads of Leviathan'. In fact,

---

23 The word 'devil' means 'slanderer' or 'blasphemer' in Greek (*diabolos*), and that is what he does in Revelation 13:6, '...he opened his mouth in blasphemies against God, to blaspheme His name...'

24 The word 'Satan' means 'adversary' or 'enemy' in Hebrew

there are in the Hebrew seven repetitions of the word 'You'[25]
— 'You divided the sea', 'You crushed the heads' and so on — perhaps depicting to us the LORD's total defeat of Leviathan in this
passage, as he has dealt with each of the seven heads.

Let us look at one more example from the Old Testament,
Isaiah 51:9.

> *Awake, awake, put on strength, O arm of the Lord;*
> *Awake as in the days of old, the generations of long ago.*
> *Was it not Thou who cut Rahab in pieces,*
> *Who pierced the dragon?*

Here 'Rahab', the power that was in Egypt, and the 'dragon' are
seen in parallel[26].

The Supernatural in Natural Terms

Why does the Bible use all these different pictures to talk about
Satan? Because otherwise, how on earth are we to talk about
something supernatural? We can talk about God because we have
seen Jesus; 'He who has seen Me has seen the Father'[27]; but how
do we talk about his enemy? We can only talk about this spiritual
being in creation terms. Just as we can only talk about 'heaven'
because of what we read about the earth in the beginning. 'God
created the heavens and the earth'[28] and then he made the sky (the
'expanse' or 'firmament'[29]) and he called it 'heaven'. So, there
is an earthly heaven (the sky) that shows us what the 'heavenly
heaven' is like — a physical one that helps us to conceive of the

---

25 Our English translations put in more 'You's!

26 There are many more references which identify Rahab with the sea
throughout the Old Testament, among them: Job 9:13; 26:12.

27 John 14:9

28 Genesis 1:1

29 Genesis 1:7

spiritual one. By calling the sky 'heaven', God gave us a language with which to talk about spiritual realities.

It is not a good idea to get too obsessed with angels and demons and spiritual beings that we cannot see and don't know too much about from Scripture. However, if God filled up the earth, we can be fairly sure that the heavens are similarly full of beings. The Bible calls them 'flames of fire', 'ministering spirits', or 'messengers'[30]. However, the 'angel' who was the chief of the angels, and who provoked a rebellion, is talked about in terms of a 'serpent', who comes into the garden; or of 'Rahab', the power behind Egypt, who was defeated as the Israelites went through the Red Sea; or of 'Leviathan', the ugly seven-headed monster; or again of 'the dragon'. This is because Satan wants to intimidate, to show off his power and to throw his weight around. Behemoth is called 'the first of the ways of God', perhaps because God's first creation was that 'angel of light' called Satan. Is that why Leviathan is seen here, in Job, as a most threatening and uncontrollable power? 'Can you draw out Leviathan with a fishhook?... Or will you bind him...?...Around his teeth there is terror...His strong scales are his pride...'[31]

If we want to understand something that is so utterly outside the realm of our normal experience, we have to talk about it in terms of more familiar things so that we can visualise it. The serpent was a picture we could understand and relate to. The devil is not, of course, literally a serpent. But he appears as such in Scripture, not as some kind of vague spirit-vapour that floats around the place - he may be like that, but that is a difficult picture to get our heads around. Thus, these are some of the different concrete pictures used in the Bible to represent Satan's cosmic spiritual force and power.

---

30 The word 'angel', in Greek *angelos,* means 'messenger' as well as angel.

31 Job 41:1-11

Whether, therefore, it is Behemoth, the 'first of all creation', or Leviathan, 'king over all the sons of pride', these are the forces of evil which are behind all suffering. They want to show that Calvary Love is not fit to run the universe by exerting the 'might is right' power of Satan. Here in Job[32], 'might is right' swishes its tail as it does in the book of Revelation[33], and its fearsome power sweeps all that is nearby to destruction. All these forces gathered together build up a picture for us of our archenemy.

Chaos and free will

The world is built on randomness because it is built out of love. The indeterminacy results from love allowing a measure of free will. But God's Word brings order to that random chaos. The chaos is also where these spiritual forces operate, because out of his great love, God gave them responsibility to administer his universe, and thus they are ultimately accountable to him.

Today, scientists observe this principle in our physical world. At the base of matter there exists indeterminacy. Particles do not obey the Newtonian physical laws of cause and effect, even though they can be contained by statistical laws. Instead they behave unpredictably. There is a sort of 'sea' of uncontrollable randomness at the most fundamental level of the world in which we live. Scientists cannot predict it; they do not know what a particle will do next at this minute level; they do not understand how particles can jump from one place to another without going through the space that is in between. The world is still very mysterious to us at this level.

The indeterminism of matter represents for us, I believe, the randomness which allows free will to exist in our universe. God set it up that way because he wanted to govern his creation by

32 Job 40:15-17
33 Revelation 12:4

love, and for love to exist we need free will to be operating in the system. This doesn't impinge on God's control of the Universe. He reigns in this realm by the statistical laws which contain the indeterminate elements. There will always be a degree of complexity that is beyond control within the system. This allows the system to be upset when beings within it steer off course. This is what happens when Satan, in his rebellion against God's system, rages through the universe, damaging the harmony and balance that God set in place. He is like a raging 'sea' that must be tamed and brought under control by the power of God. Order is restored by people exercising their free will to choose and creating a resistance to the chaos – beginning from inside them – to bring it under the discipline of the system God originally had in mind. If we were forced to sin, God would be unjust to judge us. If the source of disobedience is something outside of myself, then that is what needs to be judged. But if I make the decision—if the sea of chaos works in me and I make the choice whether or not to bring it into order by obeying God—then the source of choosing right or wrong is in me. I can legitimately be judged by God as to what I have done with the power that is working behind the scenes and within me. We can choose to be energised, helped or empowered by either the devil or God,[34] but with God's help we can do mighty things.

This is God's second answer to Job. The first reminded him of the complexity of the universe (chapters 38-39) and this second reveals the chaotic nature of the spiritual powers that exist behind the matter in which we live (chapters 40-42). The Old Testament monsters represent the hostile powers who war against God. We are those who stand on God's side, resisting these areas of warfare and disorder. Just as Jesus came to 'destroy the works

---

34 Ephesians 2:2 talks of 'the spirit that is now working in the sons of
   disobedience'; the same Greek words are used again in Ephesians
   3:20, this time talking of God's power working in us.

of the devil'[35] so we are called, alongside him, to refuse, reject, renounce, forbid and cast out the forces that would seek to bring misery, unhappiness, and the dominance of evil onto the human race.

We may never understand the individual details of suffering, the *complexity* of the random crossfire of the battle between Satan and God, in which we are sometimes caught. We may not know each specific of why this happened or why that did not happen in this life. But one day, Jesus promises us that all mysteries will be revealed.[36] Then, in the coming of Jesus' kingdom, we shall fully know what we currently only see in part, and we shall understand and be at peace. Moreover, we may not be as powerful as Leviathan, we may not feel able to contend with the mighty spiritual powers that rage around the universe, but at least we know that Satan and his minions are creatures, not an uncreated equal to God. They are creatures that God has made who have rebelled, and as such, the prophet Isaiah tell us, their end will come: 'In that day the Lord will punish Leviathan the fleeing serpent…And He will kill the dragon who lives in the sea.'[37] 'In that day' looks forward to that final eschatological moment where the kingdom of this world becomes the kingdom of our Lord and of his Christ[38]. We need to get more eschatological theology into us, so that we can live in the hope and the faith of that day here and now.

---

35 1 John 3:8

36 Matthew 10:26

37 Isaiah 27:1

38 Revelation 11:15

11

The Fighting will not Last Forever

'I have heard of You by the hearing of the ear;
But now my eye sees You...' (Job 42:5)

A vision of Christ

What is the conclusion to the book of Job? I have declared as the title of this final chapter, that the fighting will not last forever. These are words of true and sure hope: there will be a conclusion to our suffering in this life. Even in this life, God moves us away from the frontline from time to time. Here, at the beginning of Job 42, Job has seen a vision. It is the vision of Jesus on the Cross that will sustain us too, even if we do not understand all the complications we have been going through. We see Jesus. We see him suffer with such grace, and it inspires us to stand our ground, like him, and to defy the enemy together with him. That vision is deep enough to keep us going; so that even if you were the only one left in the universe, you could still say, 'Jesus is worthy of loving, even if I get nothing out of it.' He alone is fit to sit on the throne of the universe, so no matter what happens, or what the devil throws at us, let's say 'I am on your side, Lord, for you are perfect Love.'

'Everything Job said about Me was right'

> *'Therefore I retract,*
> *And I repent...' (Job 42:6)*

Job's words here do not mean that he was sorry for some moral sin; that is not what the word 'repent' means here. It means that Job has changed his mind, rejected his previous way of thinking, and wants to be taught and to understand the ways of God as he listens to his wisdom. It is not that Job has sinned and feels sorry about it. The same word for 'repent' in Hebrew, *nacham*, is used for God changing his mind, as well as for people, so it cannot refer to regret for moral sin.[1]

> *And it came about after the LORD had spoken these words to Job, that the LORD said to Eliphaz the Temanite, 'My wrath is kindled against you and against your two friends, because you have not spoken of Me what is right as My servant Job has.' (Job 42:7)*

God uses a wonderful phrase to describe Job: 'My servant Job'. He uses it four times at the end of the book and twice at the beginning. Job was 'My servant' just as Jesus, *the* Servant of God, was called 'My Servant'[2]. It is an awesome designation, to be called, like Jesus, God's servant.

---

1   Genesis 6:6 and contrast 1 Samuel 15:29 & 15:35
2   Isaiah 52:13

God says that his servant Job has spoken of him what is right. We might think he uttered all kinds of blasphemous things about the unjust way God was treating him. But as we have seen, Job was talking about the god his friends were describing. 'If God is really like what you are saying, he is not worthy to be called God. And I never knew him like that, anyway!' says Job. Job had had a friendship with and a love for the true God. The one that Job was fighting and speaking against was Satan, although he didn't know it at the beginning. It was Satan who was afflicting him, whereas his friends with their clever theology had said it was God. So everything Job said was right.

God was pleased that Job did not believe in or even want the kind of god described by his theologian friends. He had stood and vindicated the God we see in Jesus, the only God who is fit to run the universe.

Double Portion—The 'Church of the First-Born'

> *And the Lord restored the fortunes of Job when he prayed*
> *for his friends, and the Lord increased all that Job had*
> *twofold. (Job 42:10)*

God is a giving God! The Hebrew word for 'restored'[3] here is only used in this one place in the Bible for an individual; everywhere else, it is used for a whole company of people. Job's recompense was a double one! He had twice as much of his possessions as he had before. His children were not doubled; he has the same number as before. But since he no doubt prayed for them, they are probably now with him in glory, so that works out as double too!

Whose is the double portion? It is the first-born portion. In Hebrews, we are called 'the church of the first-born'[4]. However, in

---

3 Hebrew word *shub*

4 Hebrews 12:23

Bible times, not everybody who was born first in a family actually achieved the first-born blessing.[5] If we read the book of Hebrews closely, we see that not everybody lives up to what they are meant to be as Christians, either. I want to be in the 'church of the first-born, among those of the double portion in the glory! Not because I want to be the best (I hope), but because it will give joy to God to have a 'first-born church'. He wants to give a double portion to those who have stood their ground for him through their lives. Job was the forerunner, or the type, of all the first-born sons of the first-born church. He is pointing forward to the day when Jesus tells us some are given ten cities, some five, and some get none[6]. There are those who 'enter into the joy of their Lord', and others who weep and gnash their teeth - they forfeit or lose something, and therefore grieve over that loss[7].

Jesus tells a parable of ten virgins[8]. Five go into the wedding feast and five are left outside. The Lord looks out into the dark-ness at midnight and says to them, 'I don't know who you are!' The kingdom is like the *ten* virgins, not just the five who 'got in'. There will be those who go into the wedding feast and reign with Christ, and those who, sadly, will not. The first-born church will feast and reign with Christ through the ages.

This last word to Job is an indication that God has a full life for us. Those who stand their ground in pressured moments bring glory to God. They will come through into a place where they are not left, or forgotten. They will be those of whom it is said that despite the sufferings of this present age, the glory that shall be revealed to them will far outweigh the sufferings[9].

---

5   cf Genesis 25:25, 33-34; 49:3, 4; 1 Chronicles 5:1-2

6   Luke 19:12-26

7   The same parable in Matthew 25:14-30

8   Matthew 25:1-13

9   Romans 8:18

> *The Spirit Himself testifies with our spirit that we are children of God, **but**[10] if children, heirs **also**[11], **on the one hand** heirs of God, **on the other hand**[12] joint heirs with Christ, if we suffer with Him, that we may be glorified together with Him. (Romans 8:16-17 Translation mine)*

We are all heirs of God's kingdom, but if we are those who suffer with Christ, then we are 'fellow heirs' with Christ, the First-Born, and so we share his first-born status. We are all children, but we want to be those who suffer and endure with Christ, so that we go on to reign with Christ. I want to live up to my first-born status. I want to win the prize, which Paul said that he had not yet won in Philippians[13], but then in 2 Timothy[14], at the end of his life, he knew that he had. I want to be the sort of person who has ten or five cities, not one who lost them all. I want to be alongside Job, who endured and was called 'patient' in the New Testament[15]! I want to bring a bit of joy to God. Not just, for selfishness' sake, because it will make me feel good about myself, but because it will make God feel good; like a parent at the school prize-giving, glowing over what their son or daughter has achieved. Our heavenly Father will have wonderful joy over us on his great prize-giving day! He, too, will say, 'That's my son! That's my servant Job, or Charlie, or Beatrice' (or whoever you are)— 'They endured; they won the prize; they have the double-portion!'

That's what I'm running for? Are you? Let's not grow weary and lose heart in our sufferings; let's run for that prize together!

---

10 Greek *de*

11 Greek *kai*

12 Greek *men...de*

13 Philippians 3:12

14 2 Timothy 4:8

15 James 5:11

Appendix

Job Satisfaction

A while back someone I know had a job which he absolutely adored. This job was great. This job made him really happy, really fulfilled, and in the right sense, proud.

But one day, someone confronted him and said, "It's no wonder you love your job, because your job's too safe, too cushioned, not out there in the real world, just cocooned in a nice comfortable shelter away from where it really hurts. In fact, there are so many perks attached you've probably forgotten what your job is really like."

And he challenged him to find out! He dared him to take all the padding away, to remove all the perks, "Find out why you're so proud, take your job down to the very core, then you'll see through the whole façade; then you'll find out what your job's *really* like."

So he did. Because he wanted to know. He stripped away everything that was comfortable; all the benefits that had accrued in the years that he'd been with his job. And it's only fair to say that, for a good while, things were hard, things took some getting used to, after all, it was a dangerous thing to risk. This new job – the change was that drastic – could have really disappointed; could've really turned sour on him. He had to face the possibility that it might have been true – that he might have only loved his job because of all the perks.

For a while things seemed to be in the balance, but gradually the true nature of his job began to emerge, and the more it came out the more he realised, "Yes, I know now why I so enjoy my job." And it was true! His job was still exactly what he wanted. In fact, by taking all the luxuries away his job somehow became even better: refined, refocused, with a new momentum that completely dwarfed all the previous successes.

And the one who challenged him – claiming that he only loved his job for all the fringe benefits – had to admit, "Yes, your job is great, your job is all anyone could ask for."

And so my friend was even more proud of his job than before. He couldn't stop talking about his job and spent many more contented years finding ways of expressing his true character through his job.

Director's note: Now change each "j" from each "job" into a capital "J" and see how this changes the way you read the story.

© Rob Lacey

Used with permission.